A User's Guide to Therapy

A USER'S GUIDE
to THERAPY

What to Expect &
How You Can Benefit

TAMARA L. KAISER

W. W. NORTON & COMPANY
New York • London

For information about permission to reproduce selections from this book,
write to Permissions,
W. W. Norton & Company, Inc., 500 Fifth Avenue, New York, NY 10110

For information about special discounts for bulk purchases, please contact
W. W. Norton Special Sales at specialsales@wwnorton.com or 800-233-4830

Manufacturing by Quebecor World Fairfield Graphics
Production manager: Leeann Graham

Library of Congress Cataloging-in-Publication Data

Kaiser, Tamara L., 1948–
   A user's guide to therapy : what to expect and how you can benefit /
Tamara L. Kaiser. — 1st ed.
        p.   cm.
   Includes bibliographical references and index.
   ISBN 978-0-393-70534-8 (pbk.)
   1. Psychotherapy—Popular works. 2. Psychotherapy patients. I. Title.
   RC480.515.K35   2008
   616.89'14—dc22   2008017092

W. W. Norton & Company, Inc., 500 Fifth Avenue, New York, N.Y. 10110
www.wwnorton.com

W. W. Norton & Company Ltd., Castle House, 75/76 Wells Street, London
W1T 3QT

1 2 3 4 5 6 7 8 9 0

For
Cecil Bear

CONTENTS

ACKNOWLEDGMENTS

It has been a joy to have the opportunity to write a book for psychotherapy clients (and potential clients) about a process I deeply believe in and to which I have devoted every aspect of my career. I am very grateful to Michael McGandy and Deborah Malmud at Norton Professional Books for initiating and encouraging this project, and to my colleague Pauline Boss for recommending me to Michael. I offer a big thank you to Deborah for challenging me to rethink and rewrite in ways that added much to the book.

Many teachers and colleagues have helped me deepen my understanding of how to do this work. I especially want to thank Ron Johnson and Peg Thompson, from whom I first learned the importance and value of the therapeutic process. I also thank my colleagues, as well as the clients of other therapists, who agreed to let me interview them so that the book could include their voices along with my own. I greatly appreciate their willingness to share their wisdom. I also owe much to my students as well as to those colleagues for whom I have provided supervision or consultation. They all helped me learn how to teach others about psychotherapy.

I am extremely fortunate to have many generous and talented friends, colleagues, and relatives who enabled me make the best book I could make. First, I want to thank my friend Scott Edelstein for his support and invaluable insights and suggestions regarding the development of this book. My friends and professional colleagues Linda Budd, Beverly Caruso, and Brier Miller read an early draft and gave me excellent feedback and ideas. They all put up with numerous e-mails and phone calls, generously helping me think out loud and agreeing to reread various sections. My colleagues Bill Doherty and David Roseborough and my friend Richard Snyder also read the manuscript and gave me very valuable feedback.

I also thank my friend Natalie Goldberg, who has been a mentor and a true support to me as a writer in general and for this project in particular.

My husband Erik Storlie, my sister Rebecca Gibson, my son Mark Levenstein, and my cousin Sarah Hyams—all writers themselves and each with their own perspective on the therapeutic process—not only listened to, discussed with, and supported me during moments of doubt, but also thoughtfully edited the book at various points in its development. Each one shone the light on things to think about, reconsider, and (often) rewrite. I thank especially Erik for his constant loving belief in me and in my project and for his patience with my early mornings and late nights at the computer.

Many other family members, friends, and colleagues cheered me on. Thank you especially to my daughter Ghita Carroll, and also to my stepchildren Scott Storlie and Katie Rauk, my cousins Tema Silk, David Kaiser, and Bob Kaiser, my friends Barbara Booth, Melanie McIntosh, Gay Moldow,

Lynn Richardson, Toni Silver, and (once again) my colleague Pauline Boss. Thank you to my colleagues in the College of St. Catherine/University of St. Thomas School of Social Work who offered support and enthusiasm and took on some of my duties while I was on sabbatical to do this project. Thank you, as well, to Shannon Ristau and Kathy Mandy, both of whom transcribed interviews I conducted in preparation for writing the book. Also thank you to those in the Minnesota Society for Clinical Social Work who responded to various questions I asked them during the course of my work.

Finally, I want to express my very deep gratitude to all of the people throughout the years who have let me into their hearts and allowed me to work with them as their therapist.

A User's Guide to Therapy

CHAPTER 1

Welcome to Psychotherapy

Congratulations!

You have decided to embark on a fascinating journey. Quite naturally, anyone new to psychotherapy is unsure about what, exactly, it is, and, most important, how it works. This book will help you understand just what you're getting into and how to make the best use of the experience. We'll talk about the various approaches to therapy and the terrain of the therapeutic relationship—what the role of the therapist is, what you bring to the process, and how your contribution affects what happens.

This book is based on my 35 years of experience doing therapy, and teaching others how to do it. Throughout, I use stories to illustrate the ideas I discuss. In some cases I have specific permission to use stories about my own clients or people I interviewed regarding their experience with therapy. Of course, all of the names and many personal details have been changed to protect people's privacy. In other cases the stories are compilations drawn from my experience. They all give a realistic picture of what can happen in therapy. Sometimes I'll talk about a person only once. In other cases, I'll return to people whose stories I introduced earlier, giving you a deeper picture of how the process works.

WHAT DOES PSYCHOTHERAPY MEAN?

The word *therapy* comes from the Greek word *therapeia,* which means "to take care of." Psychotherapy means taking care of the psyche—healing the human mind and spirit.

Within the realm of psychotherapy there are many different approaches. Some therapies heal the psyche but don't involve much talking—for example, therapeutic bodywork, art therapy, and energy work such as healing touch. This book is about what a colleague of Sigmund Freud aptly called "the talking cure."[1] It is, literally, a conversation between therapists and their clients. This conversation is healing because of its actual content and because of the nature of the relationship within which it occurs.

There are many types of talk psychotherapy. The specific nature of your conversation will depend on the type of approach your therapist uses and on his or her personal style. You may be given exercises or specific tasks to complete, or you may just talk. You may have a clearly set agenda for each session, and even a predictable order for how you address the topic at hand, or your conversation may be unstructured. Your therapist may guide you in a directive fashion or be nondirective, letting you take most, if not all, of the lead in terms of what you talk about and how. Later in the book we'll look at the four general kinds of talk therapy approaches in more detail.

"Ok, I'm Here, but I'm Still Not Sold"

Even if you've already made the decision to start therapy, it's natural to have some doubts about doing so, both at the beginning of the process and along the road, as you hit difficult stretches. Many of us have a mental list of what kind of people go to therapy, and often that list doesn't include us. Perhaps you have such a list. Therapy is for rich people. Therapy is for poor people. Therapy is for white people. Therapy is for crazy people. Therapy is for people who can't figure out things on their own, or who don't have the kinds of friends or family who can help them when they need it. Therapy is for people who are self-indulgent and spend too much time worrying about themselves. Therapy is for people who don't believe in God or who lack a spiritual path. Therapy is for touchy-feely people. Therapy is for weak people. Therapy is for people who lack loyalty to their family or community. Therapy is for people who are part of mainstream society. Therapy is for people who aren't part of mainstream society.

In fact, like exercise and massage, *therapy is for anyone who can benefit from it.*

Making the decision to begin therapy takes courage on your part. Let's define *courage* as doing something that you believe is good to do, even if you're scared. Yes, therapy might seem scary, especially at first. You've decided to talk to a perfect stranger about things that are entirely personal. You don't know how she will react and you don't know what you will learn.

Some people are hesitant to go to therapy because they are afraid they will find out something about themselves that they don't like. Or they are afraid they will learn something about their important relationships that they don't like. Both of these fears are reasonable. When people enter therapy they examine deeply held assumptions and beliefs and sometimes choose to make profound changes as a result of what they learn. However, the important word here is *choose*. The goal of therapy is not to make you change in ways that don't work for you. Rather, the goal is to raise your awareness about who you are, what your life is all about, and how you relate to yourself and the world. The goal of any therapy, however, does include change. Sometimes the most significant change we can make is in coming to accept ourselves and our situations just as they are. However, if you see no need for change, then there's no benefit in going to therapy.

What's Special about Psychotherapy?

Certainly there are many very effective ways to get help for a problem or simply to learn to live a fuller, more aware life. Most of us have friends, family, clergy, teachers, or others in our lives from whom we seek advice, an outside opinion, or an opportunity just to let off some steam. Many of us find that we get a lot out of looking inward for direction, using spirituality and religion to serve as a guide as we encounter challenges in our lives.

Psychotherapy is not, of course, the only way to get help, but it does have characteristics that are hard to find in most other situations. Let's look at some of these.

A ONE-WAY STREET

Your relationship with your therapist is one way: The whole purpose of the therapeutic relationship is to help you do whatever personal work you came to do. Your relationship with a clergy person or teacher usually includes an expectation that you learn something specific or that you have a particular set of values. When you're with a friend or family member, you generally expect to attend to his feelings, desires, needs, and agendas as much as he attends to yours. This might mean that even though you have something important to talk about, if your friend is too tired or busy to listen or has something equally important on his mind, you may decide not to bring it up. It might also mean that you watch what you say for fear of upsetting him or for fear that he might think ill of you. You don't have to worry about your therapist in the same way. You don't have to be concerned that what you say, feel, or think will upset him. His only job is to respond in ways that are helpful to you. Of course, your therapist is human and will have his own reactions, but you can expect him to take care of himself and, if necessary, to seek help in dealing with those reactions through professional consultation with his supervisor or colleagues or through his own therapy.

It's important to realize that your therapist's responses to you won't follow the social rules and conventions that we observe in other relationships. For example, Bob told his client Rachel that, although she frequently asked him for suggestions and support, she generally found reasons to reject them. He told her that this left him feeling frustrated. He then invited her to explore with him what might be behind her behavior, as well as her feelings about his reaction to it. He did not want her to behave in a different way so that he would feel more comfortable. Rather, he raised the issue because he thought a conversation about it would help her learn something about herself.

Of course, we do sometimes give friends and family feedback to help them understand something about themselves or figure out something. But we often do so because we want them to know their impact on us. We may want them to change their behavior because we don't like it or to continue what they're doing because we like it. In addition, social convention often requires us not to challenge them and to simply enjoy (or endure) their company.

The one-way nature of the therapy process does not mean that only one of you is doing the work. Therapy is a team effort. Your therapist has an important job and so do you. But the focus of both of your jobs is on *you*—your growth, your change, your life challenges.

EDUCATION AND TRAINING FOR PSYCHOTHERAPISTS

Psychotherapists are professionals who have completed a particular type of education and training that is very rigorous and is different from others who offer counseling, such as clergy or spiritual directors. Friends, family members, and community leaders don't necessarily have any training in counseling others. This fact doesn't make them less wise or helpful, but it does mean that they don't necessarily know the same kinds of things that a psychotherapist knows.

You will find practicing psychotherapists who come from the professions of clinical social work, marriage and family therapy, psychology, professional counseling, nursing, and psychiatry. Social workers, marriage and family therapists, professional counselors, and nurses have earned, at minimum, master's degrees. Psychologists have earned Ph.D.s or Psy.D.s and psychiatrists, M.D. degrees. In most states, all need a license or some other state-sanctioned certification to practice. The standards for obtaining the certification vary from state to state. For example, in some states psychologists are permitted to prescribe medications, provided they have obtained the requisite training. In addition, all licensed or certified mental health professionals are required to continue to gain knowledge through attending workshops, earning certifications, or engaging in other specific (and sometimes in-depth) training.

There is a basic body of knowledge and set of skills that a person must learn in order to provide mental health counseling, and all professionals have training in those basics. Here are some things you can assume your therapist has learned, no matter what type of degree she earned or what postgraduate training she has pursued:

- How humans develop: how and at what stage of life people learn to process the situations they encounter.
- How relationships work: those between parents and children and those between friends and between intimate partners.
- How people with various personality types tend to view and respond to the world.
- Characteristics and challenges of mental conditions such as depression and anxiety.
- Skills in assessing a client's situation and making a plan for how to address it.

- One or more of four general therapeutic approaches: psychodynamic, cognitive–behavioral, humanistic, and family systems theories (which I describe in Chapter Six).
- All know about the workings of individual therapy and many also know about family and group therapy (all of which I discuss in Chapter Seven).

Depending on the type of graduate degree the professional earned and the particular graduate program he or she attended, certain topics may have received more emphasis. Here is a very general (and incomplete) list of some of those differences in emphasis.

- Clinical social workers learn about individuals' internal processes and their social interactions and also emphasize the context of the environment, including families, communities, and larger social and economic conditions.
- The education for marriage and family therapists emphasizes how family members interact with one another and how family dynamics affect each individual, but also includes attention to internal processes. In more recent years their education has also included attention to the larger social environment.
- Professional counselors have earned a master's degree in counseling or in another mental health field (such as psychology). The specific degree will vary in emphasis, but all will contain the general areas of knowledge necessary to practice therapy. Many contain content on vocational or career counseling.
- Psychologists learn first about individuals' internal thinking and emotional processes, with an emphasis on diagnosis,

assessment (including, for some psychologists, psychological testing) and treatment planning, and then are required to develop further areas of specialty, some of which they learn while in their graduate programs.

- Psychiatrists and clinical nurse specialists are trained in understanding how biological processes affect mental health. All psychiatrists and some clinical nurse specialists also know how psychotropic medications (that is, medications that affect mood and thinking processes) work, when they will be useful, and which ones are most appropriate for any one individual.

Each professional's postgraduate training is unique. You may find that your therapist has in-depth knowledge about a specific issue such as divorce, depression, or grief, or a specific population of clients, such as Latino, child, or gay. She may have training in a specialized form of treatment, such as sex therapy, used to treat people with sexual dysfunctions (for example, the inability to achieve an erection or to have an orgasm). She may also be well-versed in some of the areas of focus emphasized more strongly in another professional's graduate education. Some therapeutic processes require a certain kind of professional training. For example, only psychiatrists and trained clinical nurse specialists (and, in a few states, trained psychologists) can prescribe medicine, and only trained psychologists can perform psychological testing. However, a social worker or marriage and family therapist may know a lot about how medicines work or what certain psychological tests mean, perhaps because of courses she took after she completed her degree.

PROFESSIONAL ETHICS

Unless you live in a small community or are part of a closely knit cultural group, it's likely that your psychotherapist will not be part of your regular life. All mental health professions have codes of ethics that guide their behavior. One guideline prohibits dual relationships, that is, having more than one type of relationship with a client. For example, if your therapist confided in you or asked for your advice, he would be engaging in a dual relationship, turning you into a friend or consultant rather than a client.

Of course, it's not always possible to avoid all dual relationships. If you work at the only hardware store in town, your therapist may be a customer there. Even in a large community, you might run into him out in the world and might even belong to the same fitness club or have children who attend the same school. This is fine; you don't need to switch schools or fitness clubs. However, your therapist will work to make sure that this second relationship in no way compromises the primary one. The primary one—the therapeutic relationship—exists for you, not your therapist.

Another universal aspect of psychotherapists' codes of ethics is that your therapist will not share information about you unless she has your permission or a legal obligation to do so.[2] This confidentiality includes even letting others know that you are her client.

When you enter therapy, your therapist will give you a form that you will be asked to read and sign. This form states what type of information she will be sharing and with whom. For example, if you are paying for her services through your medical insurance, she will have to share diagnostic information and dates of service with your insurance company. If your therapist works for a clinic, her supervisor will have access to the record of your work in therapy. She may also talk with her supervisor about her work with you. If you are working with another professional, such as a psychiatrist, your therapist will ask you to sign a form specifically giving her permission to talk to that person.

To protect your confidentiality, it's a good idea to discuss with your therapist how you would like to handle situations where you run into each other in public. Here are some options:

- Your therapist will not acknowledge you unless you initiate contact by saying "hello."
- You will both say "hello" upon seeing each other but engage in no further (or only minimal and superficial) conversation. Neither of you will discuss anything related to your therapy sessions.
- If your therapist is with someone else and needs to explain who you are, she will say that you are a friend of a friend.
- You will decide on a situation-by-situation basis whether you want the others present to know this is your therapist. If you do, you will introduce her as such.
- Your therapist will let you introduce yourself to anyone she is with, so that you are free to give only your first name or even a fake name, if you'd rather do so.
- Your therapist will introduce you by a name on which the two of you have previously agreed.

Although some clients find these boundaries awkward and unnatural at first, they are actually necessary for the process of therapy to work. They provide a fence around the relationship that frees you from the kinds of things you have to consider in other relationships. That freedom allows you to say what you need to say, investigate what you need to investigate, feel what you need to feel, and learn what you need to learn, without the usual concerns about how the process will affect someone else. This ability and this freedom open the door for you to get to know yourself in ways that might not have felt possible before—perhaps even in ways that you didn't know existed.

The therapists' code of ethics also includes matters such as not practicing outside of their area of expertise, keeping accurate records, ending services when appropriate, and always acting in ways that do not harm clients.

Goals

The therapeutic process is goal oriented, and the primary goal is to enhance your well-being and growth by enabling you to gain greater awareness and increase your options for relating to yourself and to the world. This is not true of most other relationships, especially those that aren't one way. Of course, we often do grow and change as a result of our interactions with others, but it's generally not the main reason for the relationship.

You Pay for Therapy

Having to pay for therapy makes some people uncomfortable. They may worry that this means that they don't have friends or supportive family members to talk to. Or they may worry that their therapists really don't care about them and are just talking to them for the money. Neither of these beliefs is accurate. You are not paying for a friend or someone to talk to; you are paying a professional to help you deal with something in your life. Furthermore, the fact that your therapist earns his living by talking with you and others does not mean he doesn't care about you. On the contrary, a good professional relationship requires that your therapist genuinely care about who you are.

The fact that therapy costs money may affect how often and for how long you see your therapist. Insurance companies usually limit the number of therapy sessions for which they will pay or don't cover it at all (for example, some policies won't cover couple or family sessions). If you want more therapy than your policy will allow or you can't or don't want to use insurance, you will have to pay for it yourself. You might have a health savings account or flexible spending account through your work that you can use to help pay for therapy, but both of these types of accounts are limited by the amount of money that is in them. These limitations could affect the work you do in therapy. For example, you may make changes more quickly if you know you have a short time in which to do so; you may set more limited goals for yourself than you would if you had more time; you may find that you have to end therapy before you're ready; or you may come less frequently than you need or want to come.

Paying for therapy can help clarify important questions about your commitment to the process. Investing in therapy may mean spending less on something else. In a society where material goods are often equated with personal worth and happiness, some people wonder about the value of spending money on therapy. Yet therapy has the potential to improve the quality of your life far more than you can imagine.

Some people feel that they can't afford psychotherapy because they have medical costs that they consider more important. Although you certainly shouldn't skimp on necessary medical costs, many studies indicate that psychotherapy can actually improve physical health conditions, reduce costs associated with them, or at least help people cope more effectively.[3]

It's also possible that you feel selfish spending money on something that seems to benefit only you. Of course you and your family all have basic needs, such as food, shelter, and health care, that are more important than your psychotherapy. However, we often give more weight to what we think others need and deserve than to what we need and deserve. Also, it's important to remember that the changes you make in therapy are likely to positively affect others about whom you care.

In this book, we will look at what makes therapy work, various types of therapeutic approaches, what you bring to the process, and what the relationship between you and your therapist is all about. Although the process of psychotherapy has a beginning, middle, and end, the journey is not a linear one that moves predictably from one point to the next. I encourage you to visualize it more like a spiral, where you meet aspects of yourself again and again, each time gaining a new or more complex awareness of who you are and how you want to be in the world.

I welcome you to join me as we look more closely at the adventure of psychotherapy.

CHAPTER 2

What Makes Therapy Work?

The Common Factors

More than 60 years of research on psychotherapy, including studies on many approaches to therapy, show that therapy works.[1] People who go to therapy to get help with their problems are, in fact, generally better off than those who don't. But what method of therapy should you choose? There are at least 200 different approaches to treatment and 400 different strategies or techniques.[2] And, of course, every therapist has his or her own unique personality and style.

Believe it or not, the specific type of therapy you choose is only one piece of the therapeutic puzzle. We now know that there are four factors that have the most impact on how much therapy helps someone:

- The client and extratherapeutic factors (things that occur outside the therapy) account for approximately 40% of change.
- The relationship between client and therapist accounts for about 30%.
- Hope and the expectation that therapy will work account for about 15%.

- The particular techniques used in therapy account for about 15%.

Common Factor #1 (40%): The You Factor[3]

People develop various processes for learning about themselves and for changing, all of which occur in the natural course of living. We experience our lives; we think about our situations; we express our thoughts and feelings; we tell our stories; we get feedback from others; we try out and evaluate new ideas and new ways of behaving. Therapy helps to jumpstart and focus these processes. Therapists don't change people; rather, *people change themselves with the help of therapy*.

Once in therapy, clients' success depends a lot on how they engage in the process and what they bring to it. Many studies confirm that those who are open to the process, as well as those who *work together* with their therapists rather than depending on them, tend to get more out of therapy. Clients who are highly motivated and those who have a clear sense of what they want to address also get more from the process. Nevertheless, some issues may lend themselves to a more rapid change, whereas others may take longer.

Common Factor #2 (30%): You and Your Therapist[4]

The quality of the relationship between clients and therapists is a major contributor to the success of therapy. Many clients report that the most helpful aspect of therapy is simply having the space to reflect solely on themselves— something that many of us don't have much opportunity to do. This unique focus is possible because of the one-way nature of the relationship. Other clients most value having someone who listens to them, understands who they are, gives them suggestions, and supports them.

What you bring to the relationship, of course, affects how you experience your therapist and how the process works for you. For example, if you expect people in authority to tell you what to do, you may expect this of your therapist and feel uncomfortable when she encourages you to find your own answers. You will learn a lot simply by looking at how you respond to your therapist.

Your relationship with your therapist offers you important opportunities. First, it provides you with a person who is devoted to thinking about your life with you. You can talk out loud about your situation, gain another's perspective, and gain distance by standing with your therapist and looking at yourself. Second, because we see our relationships through the lens of our life experiences, in our relationship with a therapist we can relive and reexamine some of the experiences we have had with others.

In addition, the relationship can serve as a healing experience. From the quality of the interactions with your therapist, you can learn what it's like to have someone listen to you fully, challenge you effectively, respond to you genuinely, offer deep compassion, and respectfully help you address any conflicts and misunderstandings that may occur in the relationship.

Here's an example of an interaction between a therapist and client about their relationship. Recall Rachel from Chapter One, who asked for, and then rejected, her therapist's support and suggestions. Rachel and Bob, her therapist, had the following conversation about her reluctance to tell her husband that she'd like more help with their children:

Rachel: But if I try to talk to my husband, he'll just ignore me.

Bob: What makes you think that's what will happen?

Rachel: He just comes home every night and turns on the TV. No matter what's going on around him, he just tunes it out—stares at that tube.

Bob: What do you say to yourself when he does that?

Rachel: I just know there's no point. Besides, he's tired. And anyway, he gets impatient with the kids, so he really isn't much of a help.

Bob: Sounds like you might be ambivalent about whether you really want his help, or whether it's okay to ask him for it.

Rachel: That's not true. I just don't think he'll do it. He's never been much of a help.

Bob: I wonder if it seems pretty hopeless.

Rachel: Not exactly. I know I can handle the kids on my own. And he's a good provider. And a good guy. It's just that sometimes I wish he'd be more involved.

Bob: I guess I meant you might feel hopeless about being able to get more of what you want from him. Is that true?

Rachel: Well, kind of. But like I said, I probably get more than a lot of women. My friends all complain about the same thing. And sometimes their husbands don't even come home till late. So maybe I'm just being unrealistic.

Bob: It could be. But I'm wondering if it's hard for you to give yourself permission to ask for help.

Rachel: I don't think so. I ask my kids to help with chores and stuff.

After a few more attempts to help Rachel get to the bottom of this issue, Bob was beginning to feel frustrated—not a new feeling in his work with this client. He and Rachel had had several such conversations in the past. He decided to address the interaction between them more directly.

Bob: I'm noticing that in this conversation today, you seem to be responding to many of my ideas with a "yes—but." Do you know what I mean by that?

Rachel: Not really.

Bob: Well, it seems like you have lots of reasons why nothing will really work to resolve your frustration that your husband doesn't help with the kids. Anything I suggest that might help us understand what you're feeling and thinking sounds like it's not really hitting the mark. It feels like we're running into a lot of dead ends. Does it feel that way to you—or just to me?

Rachel: Yeah . . . maybe. I guess so.

Bob: I'm wondering how it feels to hear me describe it this way.

Rachel: I don't know . . . I guess I feel really frustrated. I just don't know what to do. Nothing seems right.

Bob: That *is* frustrating. I'm actually starting to feel a bit frustrated myself. I'm wondering if we can talk more about how stuck you must feel.

Rachel: I'm sorry, I can't help it.

Bob: When you say you're sorry, it sounds like you're worried about how I might be reacting to you. Is that right?

Rachel: Well, I don't know how to keep you from being frustrated. I'm not trying to be difficult.

Bob: Remember we talked early on about the fact that I might sometimes bring up how I'm experiencing you in the sessions?

Rachel: Yeah . . .

Bob: Remember how I said I wouldn't be doing that to get you to take care
          of me? I know you're not trying to frustrate me, and I'm not worried
          about the fact that I'm feeling that way. It's okay that I'm frustrated,
          and I don't need you to do anything for me about that feeling. But I
          think my feelings and yours might give us some good information. I'm
          bringing this up because I think there's something really important
          going on, and I think we can learn something by talking about it.

Rachel: Well, actually, it sort of scares me when you say you're frustrated.
          I'm scared that you don't want to work with me anymore.

Bob: That would be scary. It's not true. I do very much want to work with
          you. But I'm really glad that you told me you're scared of that. Let's
          see if we can look at this a little more. What makes you think that if
          I say I'm frustrated, I might want to stop working with you?

Rachel: Well, if you're frustrated, and we're just hitting dead ends, you
          can't help me.

Bob: That's a big conclusion. How did you get there?

Rachel: I just think I must be hopeless. No one can help. See, even you're
          giving up. Everyone does.

Bob: Wow. That must be a hard way to feel about yourself. I wonder if we
          could talk more about your experience of people giving up on you?

Rachel: Well, yeah . . . it seems like I've always had to do everything for my-
          self. You know how I was always in charge of my little brothers.

Bob: I remember you told me in our first or second session that both your
          parents drank a lot. I'm thinking this had a lot to do with your feel-
          ings of being alone. It's pretty impossible for parents to take care of
          their kids if they're drunk!

Rachel: I guess that's true. But they were always at home. It's not like they
          went to the bars or anything. But now that you mention it, they
          sure weren't paying attention to us.

Bob: That sounds like how you describe your husband now.

Rachel: Well, but he never drinks. That's one of the things I've always
          liked about him.

Bob: That makes it confusing, I bet. He's not doing the obvious thing that
        made your parents unavailable.

As their conversation continued, Rachel saw that, because of her experiences in past relationships, she both feared and expected that her therapist would not be available to help her. Furthermore, she realized that her behavior with Bob actually invited that very reaction from him. She also discovered that she believed she really didn't deserve any help. If she succeeded in discouraging Bob, she would fulfill her expectations and confirm her own beliefs.

Bob's response was a new and healing one for Rachel. She learned that he was willing to stick with her in spite of her unconscious attempts to push him away, thus communicating that he wanted to help and that she deserved that help. She agreed, though somewhat reluctantly, to an experiment. Sometime before their next session, she would ask her husband to help with something small—maybe just to look over the announcements the school sent home that day—and see how he responded.

COMMON FACTOR #3 (15%): "I THINK THIS IS GOING TO WORK!"[5]

Without a sense that therapy can help, you're unlikely to even want to begin. But you don't need complete confidence in your therapist or in the process, just some hope that it might make a positive difference.

Simply taking the step of making an appointment can give you a sense of hope. Your therapist's confidence in himself and in you can also give you hope, because he believes that he can help you and, more importantly, he believes that you have the ability to benefit from the process.

Your therapist's confidence includes his attitude about his approach to the work. That is, he has a theoretical perspective and a way of doing things in which he believes and trusts. If you also find his take on things both believable and useful, you will begin to feel hopeful that there's a way to understand yourself, to generate helpful ideas, and to act on them.

Common Factor #4 (15%): Techniques[6]

Although the general goal of all therapies is for clients to think, act, or feel in ways that are helpful to them, there are many paths to that goal. Your therapist's paths need to work for you. The fact is, what will work for some clients won't necessarily work for others. There is evidence that certain techniques are particularly useful for certain problems. For example, relaxing each muscle as you focus on your body, starting from one end and moving to the other, has been found to help people reduce anxiety.[7] However, what's most important is what your therapist does to help you deal with your situation. Your therapist's way of understanding and helping people needs to make sense to you.

Rachel was encouraged by the results of her therapist Bob's technique of discussing their interactions with one another. Rather than continuing to feel her familiar sense of frustration and helplessness, Rachel saw something new and positive happen. This change gave her hope that he could help her change other aspects of her life as well.

Although the common factors—the client, the therapeutic relationship, the client's hope, and the therapist's technique—sound like four separate categories, they are deeply interrelated. Each supports the other, and strengthening any one can help make the others more effective as well.

CHAPTER 3

What Makes Therapy Work?

Psychotherapy and the Brain

There is an inescapable connection between the brain and psychotherapy because our experiences shape the way our brains develop and function. Let me offer a brief, if oversimplified, explanation of this connection, taken from Louis Cozolino's *The Neuroscience of Psychotherapy*.[1]

This explanation must be greatly simplified because the brain is an extremely complex organ and neuroscience is a rapidly growing field comprised of several scientific disciplines. With new technology, researchers can watch what is happening in the brain and see changes in its structure or functions that correlate with feelings, thinking, and behavior. One discovery, for example, shows that if a tiny part of the brain, the insula, is damaged in smokers, they lose their urge to smoke. Another reveals the impact of an increase or decrease of the hormone oxytocin on a person's desire and ability to nurture, trust, and bond with others.[2] It's a fascinating topic that is far too vast to cover adequately in a single book, much less a short chapter. Nevertheless, this review will help you understand something important about why psychotherapy works.

THE BRAIN'S THREE MAJOR PARTS

In the 1970s a pioneering neuroscientist named Paul MacLean suggested that the brain is divided into three basic parts: the brainstem, cortex, and limbic system. Although we now know that this does not fully express the brain's complexity, it's a good starting point.

These three parts are influenced by one another in multiple ways. Furthermore, not only the three parts, but also the right and left sides of the brain, have specialized areas of functioning. Specific areas within each side and each layer handle still more specialized functions.

The *brainstem*, located at the base of the skull above the spinal nerve, looks similar in all reptiles and mammals and is fully functioning when a child is born. It is responsible for automatic body functions such as breathing, heart rate, and temperature regulation, and for basic reflexes such as swallowing.

The *cortex*, the walnut-shaped grey matter that we see in pictures of the brain, is responsible for our most uniquely human capacity—our conscious self-awareness. It allows us to understand what our experience means and how to respond to it effectively. The cortex, and in particular the area of the cortex called the prefrontal cortex, is called the executive brain. It is in charge of the ways we respond to ourselves and others.

Unlike the brainstem, the prefrontal cortex develops slowly over the first 20–30 years of life. Because of this slow development, it is the part of the brain that is most affected by the environment, including interactions with the people who are emotionally and physically closest to us. It is also the part of the brain most affected by the messages we get from the media and from society as a whole, especially when we are young.

The *limbic* system lies between the cortex and the brain-stem and begins developing soon after birth. Its primary function is to ensure our survival. Although it develops more quickly than the cortex, it also is strongly affected by the environment. The limbic system is responsible for memory, learning, and emotion. Significant aspects of our early experience are stored here. Much of how we respond to life comes from our limbic system. We are strongly influenced, and sometimes even controlled, by memories and emotions deep in our limbic brains. An example: A baby hears a loud and threatening noise and reacts with terror. The noise is registered in the limbic system, which makes no distinction between the popping of a big balloon and a life-threatening event. For many years afterward, when the baby grows up, he is easily startled by loud noises, even though he doesn't know why. All of us have limbic memories of early events, both positive and negative, that evoked—and continue to evoke—strong emotional responses. These stick with us, often bypassing the influence of our prefrontal cortex.

Neurons

The brain consists of billions of microscopic neurons that connect with each other, forming trillions of neural networks. Each area of the brain is a network of neurons organized to perform certain tasks. These networks create every aspect of our experience, from simple reflexes to complex and sophisticated combinations of thinking, feeling, and behavior. Over time, the brain grows and changes in response to the environment through the growth of new neurons, as well as through continued connections and reconnections among them. The brain's ability to grow and change, and the creation of larger and more complex neural networks, is called *plasticity*.

THE BRAIN AND RISK

The optimal environment for brain growth and development is one that is complicated enough to require new learning and safe enough to encourage a person to risk taking on new challenges. When everything around us is comfortably familiar, we are completely relaxed and there's no challenge to figure out how to deal with what's in front of us. We may go on "automatic pilot." But when faced with new situations, we experience some degree of stress in the form of strong emotions or physical sensations. Stress helps to focus the brain on solving this new problem—that is, on stimulating growth and new connections among neurons. If we face little or no challenge, we can't learn and grow. However, too much stress also prevents learning. In those situations our brains shut down, protecting us from becoming overwhelmed.

Much research shows that when children are securely attached to, and adequately nurtured by, the adults who raise them, they feel safe in the world and are more willing to risk new challenges.[3] Thus, secure attachment and adequate nurturing are important ingredients in an optimal learning environment. Over time children who feel safe learn to tolerate and modulate increasing levels of stress. Their care-takers soothe them when they become overwhelmed, and, as they grow older, they learn to seek soothing from others and to soothe themselves. Adults also need to feel safe in order to learn to tolerate stress and take on new challenges.

The Connection Between the Brain and Psychotherapy

The brain functions that are most relevant to psychotherapy are those related to *cognition*—that is, to the knowledge that we acquire through reasoning, intuition, perception, and *feelings*—which include both emotions and sensations. Both cognition and feelings lead to behavior. Psychological well-being requires a strong connection between our conscious cognitive abilities and our emotions and sensations. This connection helps us act in a constructive manner. In the language of brain science, we depend on the connections among the neural networks in the brainstem, limbic, and cortex systems that underlie the functions of thinking, feeling, and behavior.

We know that people who have experienced trauma in the past often react to extreme stress by dissociating—that is, by disrupting (or, in the case of children, never developing) connections among the three types of brain function. A classic example is the war veteran struggling with posttraumatic stress disorder. Many vets react with terror to a loud noise, sometimes trying to escape the danger, sometimes responding with aggression. They are unable to register on a rational level that this noise is from a car backfiring, not a hand grenade.

Even those of us who have experienced far smaller traumas can remember times when we shut down in fear (due to a disconnect in the prefrontal cortex) and we reacted irrationally, from a strong, undigested emotion associated with some memory. An example of this is my client Damian, whose parents were often extremely angry with each other, with him, and with his brother. The household was filled with loud, nasty, frightening arguments. He now gets scared when his partner Jon expresses anger, even when he does so in a calm tone of voice, without threatening words or actions.

We all have developed ways to disconnect from—that is, to avoid consciously facing—aspects of ourselves or our experiences that might trigger strong anxiety. Psychodynamic therapists have developed a long list of such strategies, calling them defenses. Let's briefly consider two very common ones: *denial* and *rationalization*. Denial allows us to keep things that we don't want to face completely out of our conscious awareness (that is, it doesn't use the prefrontal cortex). For example, Jake, who is 50 pounds overweight, recently learned that he had dangerously high blood pressure. Although previously an avid athlete, he can no longer keep up with old friends who are still very active. They repeatedly express concern about his health, but Jake laughs it off and doesn't see it as a problem. He's in denial.

Because, as adults, we have an operating prefrontal cortex that often makes it hard for us to stay in complete denial, we frequently use rationalization to avoid facing a painful awareness that is starting to poke its head up. Rationalization actually requires the use of the prefrontal cortex: We reason and talk ourselves out of doing what we need to do. Of course, we have to be aware of a concern before we can think about it and work up our rationalization. In uncomfortable moments, when Jake feels vulnerable to his friends' comments about his physical condition, he tells himself that the doctor just noticed his high blood pressure at his last visit, that it must have been caused by some temporary stress he was feeling at the time, and that it will resolve on its own. Furthermore, he tells himself that his physical work as a construction worker keeps him strong.

Changing the Brain Through Psychotherapy

Because of the plastic nature of the brain, psychotherapy can serve as an ideal environment for helping people make more and stronger connections among neural networks. In this way, the process of psychotherapy literally changes the brain. This change begins in therapy with conversation, with telling our stories.

As we grow up and our prefrontal cortex develops, each of us develops a more and more complex story about what we have experienced, how we feel about it, and who we are. This story is partly unconscious or unintentional, rising more out of the limbic system than the cortex. Psychotherapy helps us develop what Cozolino calls a "language of self reflection," which enables us to become more aware of the stories we have created and to add to and revise those stories based on new information.

The process of psychotherapy, whatever the style, always has two primary goals: *greater awareness* and *more options* for relating to ourselves and to the world. It achieves these goals through several universal characteristics:

- Therapy offers the necessary safe relationship.
- Therapists help clients gain information about their experience, thereby increasing their cognitive ability in a number of ways. Therapists offer clients a conceptual framework that explains human experience, and they educate their clients about particular conditions, such as depression, sexual abuse, schizophrenia, or living in a family with an alcoholic. They also use various techniques that help raise their clients' awareness.
- Therapists encourage clients to take risks, try new ways of acting, name and communicate their emotions, and become conscious of parts of themselves that they didn't know about before, such as unaccountably strong emotions and automatic thoughts (quick, evaluative thoughts that are not the result of conscious reasoning). During this process, therapists help clients move back and forth between thoughts and feelings—a process that activates and integrates neural connections.
- Therapists help clients change their stories about who they are and how they can relate to their world when those stories are based on falsely perceived limitations.
- Therapists help clients develop strategies for making sense of their life experience once therapy is done, so that they continue to grow and integrate new learning.

So far, I've discussed some general characteristics of therapy that make it work. Now let's look at what you'll encounter when you begin the process.

CHAPTER 4

Beginning Your Therapy

Deciding which therapist to see is a difficult task. Some people choose their therapist based on the recommendation of someone they trust. Others choose based on what they can afford. Still others want to know what type of education, training, or experience their therapist has; what therapeutic approach he uses; what topics or issues she specializes in, or what groups of people he works with. Others choose based on convenience—where the therapist's office is located or whether the therapist is available at a certain time of day. All of these are reasonable variables to take into account when choosing a therapist. None, some, or all of them may be important to you. However, whichever ones matter to you, make sure that you ask about them as you decide whom to see.

Beyond these more concrete factors, it is important to feel that your therapist will be able to help you. Part of this has to do with chemistry—that inexplicable feeling of trust and connection. There is no one way to look for or discover this chemistry. However, it's often a good idea to talk with more than one therapist, either on the phone or in person, to get a sense of who would be a good fit for you before making a decision. (And, remember, if your initial choice doesn't work out, you can always see someone else.)

As you begin the selection process, there are some things that you need to find out, so that you know what to expect:

- You should know what the sessions will cost. Fees vary a great deal from professional to professional. Some therapists may offer to reduce their regular fee or use a sliding fee scale; others stick to one fee. Some therapists accept medical insurance payments; others do not.

- If you want to use your insurance, you should make sure that your therapist's services are covered under your plan and that your therapist accepts payments from that plan. To be safe, check with both the therapist (or her billing person) and the insurance company. Some plans cover only the therapists on their own provider lists; others cover anyone who has the type of license or degree that the insurance company requires. Some insurers limit the number of visits or modes of therapy (individual, family, or group) they will cover. Some require co-payments (usually $15–$25 per session).

- If you don't want to, or can't, use your insurance, you will have to pay "out of pocket." If you have some sort of medical savings account through your work, you may be able to use that money to reimburse yourself. Check with your account administrator to find out.

- You should know how and when you are expected to pay for your therapy. This includes whether you pay your co-pay and your therapist bills your insurance company; whether you pay the entire bill and then seek insurance reimbursement; and whether you pay at the end of each

session or wait for a bill. It also includes whether you will
be charged for late cancellations or missed appointments,
neither of which are covered by medical insurance.

- Finally, you should know when, where, how often, and for
how long (per session) you and your therapist will meet.
These arrangements may change as you proceed. For example, you may begin by meeting weekly and, later, meet
every other week or once a month.

"WHAT BRINGS YOU HERE?"

Both before and during the first few sessions, your therapist
is likely to ask you to talk about what is bothering you in
some detail. He might ask you to answer a series of prede-
termined questions, or he might invite you to tell your story
however you want to and then ask questions to help you
elaborate on or clarify your concerns. Exactly how and what
he asks you will depend on his style and approach and on
what records others—such as the clinic for which he works
or your insurance company—require him to keep.

Your therapist (or the clinic) may give you a form to fill
out and bring to the first or second session. The form might
ask many questions, such as whether you've experienced
anxiety or depression, whether you are on any medications,
whether you drink alcohol (and, if so, how much), whether
you've taken, or are taking, illegal drugs, whether you've
been abused, or whether anyone in your family has ever had
mental health problems. You might be asked to fill in a
genogram—a map of who is in your family. The genogram
might ask for the dates of people's births, deaths, marriages,

and divorces and for information on family members' alcoholism, depression, sexual abuse, and so on.

You might find such a form intimidating, overwhelming, or off-putting. At first, after all, you've only talked to the therapist briefly on the phone, or maybe not even done that. Now you're being asked to reveal very personal information with no real idea of what your therapist will do with it. You might feel that many of the questions aren't relevant to why you're seeking help. In contrast, some people find such a form reassuring. Perhaps there are questions about things that you wouldn't think to talk about, but are glad to be able to report. Perhaps it's easier to write things down rather than having to say them out loud. Both of these reactions are common, and neither is wrong. In fact, each tells you something about yourself—something worth paying attention to, and, ideally, something worth sharing with your therapist.

Some therapists use their initial phone conversation with a client to learn, either in great detail or briefly, what he or she hopes to gain by coming to therapy. Sondra chose to work with her therapist Mia because of the way she handled this initial phone call. Sondra had been the victim of sexual abuse by her stepfather. She had a list of several therapists and talked to each of them before deciding whom to see. Many of them asked her about her abuse experience, posing questions that Sondra found intrusive but that she felt she had to answer. She volunteered to give Mia the same information in their initial phone call, but Mia declined the offer. Instead, she said that they would talk about it if Sondra chose to see her. Sondra felt relieved and reassured by the knowledge that she would be free to reveal her history at her own pace.

But everyone is different. Some clients want to talk with a therapist at length on the phone to see how he or she responds and decide whether they want to work with that therapist further. Others prefer to give a very general idea of what they're looking for and wait until they meet the therapist to give more information.

People seek psychotherapy for many different reasons. In general, they come because they are dissatisfied with something in their life, or someone else is dissatisfied with them. They come because they want something to change, even if that something is only to change the mind of the person who thinks *they* ought to change. Sometimes people are clear and specific about what is bothering them. Other times they may have just a vague sense that life is not going the way they would like it to go. You don't need to have a specific or concrete goal. In fact, sometimes what you thought you wanted to do will not be what you end up doing. Often people find that the seemingly disparate concerns they have are connected in some way, or that there is an underlying theme.

A List of Reasons

In *Therapy Demystified,* Kate Scharff offers a long list of the kinds of things that may prompt you to go to therapy.[1]

- You feel isolated.
- You feel troubled by patterns in your personal or professional relationships.
- People suggest you should "get help."
- You suffer with an addiction (for example, to alcohol or other drugs, or to a problematic behavior such as gambling or overeating).

- You suffer from a phobia (for example you're afraid to ride elevators, fly or leave your house).
- You're grieving a loss, but people tell you that you should be "over it" by now.
- You're having trouble adjusting to a medical diagnosis or dealing with the symptoms of a medical illness.
- You have feelings of anxiety that are "free floating" (not attached to any particular situation or event).
- You have a case of the blues that never goes away, or is present too much of the time.
- You feel angry most of the time.
- You feel tired, listless, or lethargic.
- You no longer take pleasure in activities that you used to enjoy.
- You have lost interest in sex.
- You feel helpless or hopeless.
- You suffer from the irrational fear that something terrible will happen to you or someone you care about.
- You have persistent or intrusive upsetting thoughts.
- You have been assaulted or abused.
- You feel chronically disappointed in yourself and/or other people.
- You find it hard to think clearly or make decisions.
- You sleep too much or too little.
- You eat too much or too little and have lost or gained a considerable amount of weight.
- You feel grumpy or irritable.
- You don't trust your sense of yourself.
- You don't trust your sense of reality.
- You are having trouble coping or adjusting to a circumstance in your life.

- You have had thoughts of hurting yourself.
- You have had thoughts of hurting others.
- You want to die.

Naturally, no list like this can be complete. Nor is it usually the case that someone begins therapy for only one reason. You may have several concerns that you'd like to address. In general, the reasons for seeking therapy fall into two categories: problems in relationships with others and problems with your own feeling, thinking, or behavior. And, of course, some people come to therapy not because they feel the need, but because others think they should go or demand that they do.

Let's look briefly at each of these reasons.

Relationship Problems

Maybe you've noticed that you often find yourself in relationships that aren't working the way you'd like them to or think they should. Perhaps, for example, you've had difficulty keeping long-term friendships or have never been able to sustain an intimate relationship for more than a few months.

Or maybe you have concerns about a particular relationship. Adult children often seek therapy for help in resolving conflicts between themselves and their parents or other family members. Parents often ask for help raising their children or getting along with children who are now adults. Perhaps you want to make amends to your grown children for some way you hurt them when they were young, or you want to face and resolve some painful conflicts that are impeding your ability to have a satisfying adult-to-adult relationship.

Many people come to therapy because they're in an intimate relationship that isn't going as well as they would like. They may be uninterested in sex or concerned that their partner seems uninterested. They may fight about how to spend money, or how to raise their children, or how they communicate.

Some people want help deciding whether to stay in a relationship, or want to learn how to make a relationship better. Some have already ended a relationship with someone, want to come to terms with the loss, and want to learn how to avoid getting into a similar relationship in the future.

"SOMETHING ABOUT ME"

Many people come to therapy because they just don't feel right. Perhaps you find that you're irritable or sad much of the time, even though no one is really provoking you. Maybe you feel that you repeatedly fall short of your expectations of yourself and are never quite satisfied with the choices you make. Maybe you've noticed something about yourself that you can't explain but that concerns you—for example, that you're losing chunks of time and are unable to remember what happened or where you've been.

Some people want to figure out something important about their identity—for example, whether they are gay or lesbian, whether their job is really what they want to do for a living, or whether they're on the right spiritual or religious path. Some people may have already decided that they want to make a major shift in one of these areas and know that making such a shift will come with its own challenges for which they will need support.

"It's Not My Idea"

Some people come to therapy because someone else insists that they go. Often one member of a couple will want to go, and asks that the other join. Sometimes the request is an ultimatum: *"Either come with me or I'll leave."*

Often people are concerned about a friend or relative so urge her to get some help, perhaps because she seems very depressed, anxious, or stuck in her life. Perhaps your friend told you that she had done all she could to help and that you could benefit by talking to a professional. Sometimes courts order a person to go to therapy, because he has broken the law or hurt someone.

Treatment Plans

After the first couple of sessions with a client, I create a treatment plan that I share with him or her. It's a simple plan that includes what the client says brought him or her to therapy, my assessment of his or her situation, and a list of goals. Talking with the client about the plan helps ensure that we are "on the same page" as we proceed, and enables the client to evaluate how well I have understood the situation and to clarify what I may have missed. It also allows us the opportunity to talk more about what we will be doing together and to ask questions about things we don't understand. If necessary, we revise the plan together.

Although all therapists have some kind of assessment and planning process, that process can range from far more to far less detailed than mine.

UNDERSTANDING THE INITIAL ASSESSMENT

The initial assessment made by your therapist is based on information that you give him, as well as his impressions of you. It could include the strengths he sees in you, such as your ability to handle a stressful job, maintain close and supportive friendships, or make good decisions on your own and your children's behalf. It might also include areas that he thinks you could improve to help you with the issues you brought to therapy. For example, the assessment might note that the way you think is sometimes unrealistically negative or that you seem to use alcohol to cover up painful feelings. The assessment might mention things that are happening in your life that could be contributing to your current stress, such as that you recently moved, had a baby, or left an important relationship. It might also mention aspects of your personal history that could be significant—for example, that your mother died when you were in your early teens.

If you are using medical insurance to pay for your therapy, the therapist's assessment will include a mental illness diagnosis, using the *Diagnostic and Statistical Manual of Mental Disorders* (DSM IV).[2] Every medical insurance company requires a diagnosis before they will approve coverage.

There is an active and ongoing debate in the field about whether to focus in therapy on mental *illness* or mental *health*. Using medical insurance requires that you define your problem in terms of mental illness. But much of what people bring to therapy is about natural human suffering and growth, not about mental illness. The DSM-IV describes symptoms and categories of a great many mental conditions, including anxiety and depression. These conditions range from those that are relatively mild—so mild, in fact, that they might apply to any of us when we're under stress—to those that are quite serious. Even within a particular category, such as depression, diagnostic criteria for symptoms can cover a very wide range.

There are pros and cons to using the DSM-IV. Like any labeling system, this one has flaws. It's quite difficult to categorize people, and doing so runs the risk of describing people much too narrowly. Depression does not look the same in everyone who suffers from it. Nor does depression, or any other condition described in the DSM-IV, describe or explain everything about a particular human being.

However, it is important for both you and your therapist to understand, as completely as possible, what you're dealing with. If you do have a serious mental illness, knowing that you have it and what it is will help guide what you do in therapy. And if you need medication, finding the right one depends on an accurate diagnosis.

The topic of mental disorders is much too big to cover in this book. However, I encourage you to learn what you can about the diagnosis your therapist gives you. You can find good information at responsible sites on the Internet, such as MayoClinic.com. The book *Straight Talk about Your Mental Health*, by Dr. James Morrison, also offers a good overview of diagnostic categories.[3]

When I share my assessment with a client, I explain what it means. It's possible that we may disagree on the diagnosis or what it means. I am ethically bound to assess and diagnose as accurately as possible, but, again, the DSM-IV, like any classification system, is not foolproof. In some cases, there may be a diagnosis that we can both agree is close enough to describe the issue. In others, I may have to exercise my professional judgment and assign a diagnosis, even if the client disagrees.

UNDERSTANDING AND AGREEING ON GOALS

My client and I not only have to understand what our goals are in working together, we have to agree that those goals make sense. Unless both you *and* your therapist think a goal is a good one, you can't pursue it. If one of you feels strongly that the goal is essential, but the other sees it as irrelevant or even counterproductive, then you and your therapist may decide you can't work together.

Goals Your Therapist Won't Accept

You may want to set a goal for your work to which your therapist can't agree because he doesn't think it's achievable. For example, you may want to change something that is out of your control. This dilemma comes up frequently because people are often confused about who and what they can and can't control. For example, you might think "I will *finally learn how to get* my father's approval and the love I long for." Or "*I will get* my husband to stop hitting me by becoming a better wife." Recognizing our powerlessness is scary. Sometimes it's easier to believe that we can change someone else without that person's cooperation than to realize that we can only change our part—and that doing so may not be enough to make the relationship work.

On the other hand, many people believe they are *less* powerful than they really are. They focus on what they want other people to do rather than on what they can do. For example, "*If my parents had supported my dream to be*

a musician, I wouldn't be stuck in my job," or, *"If my hus-*
band stopped drinking, I'd be happy."

Although sorting out the question of who and what you
can control is typically an ongoing part of therapy, the question often arises first in the initial goal-setting phase. Your
therapist needs to be clear about what she will agree to work
on with you. For example, she can agree to help you learn to
respond to your brother more assertively, but she can't help
you *make* him respond to you in a certain way. This doesn't
mean that your own behavioral change won't affect how
your brother treats you. It does take two to tango, so if you
change your steps in the dance, or stop dancing altogether,
he can't keep doing the same steps. However, you can't control how he changes his steps, and he might change them in
a way you don't like.

Your therapist also can't agree to a goal that she can't support because of her own values or biases. She is not required to
share your values, and, as part of the one-way nature of the
relationship, she will strive to set aside her values to support
you. But there are times when she can't, with integrity, support something that goes against her own deeply held beliefs.

For example, I was once approached by a couple who
wanted me to help them have a successful open marriage—
that is, a marriage in which each could have extramarital
sexual liaisons. I became an adult in the 1960s and have observed many open marriages. I saw that, at least in this culture, such arrangements inevitably hurt someone, if not
many people. Thus I couldn't ethically support that couple's
goal, and I declined their request for my counseling.

Or consider my colleague, Mary, who is strongly opposed
to abortion. She can't fully support a pregnant client who

wants help in deciding whether or not to bring her baby to term. Instead, Mary refers such clients to someone who is not attached to whether they give birth to the child or have an abortion.

Goals You Won't Accept

Your therapist may want you to set a goal that you don't agree is relevant or necessary. For example, Polly wanted to work on her anger, which got her in trouble at work. Her therapist, Bruce, thought that her problem stemmed from unresolved anger at her parents, but Polly had no interest in exploring that area—she just wanted to stay on her employer's good side. Although they disagreed, Bruce thought that they could successfully focus on the work issue, and they agreed to continue. Perhaps Polly would change her mind down the road and add a goal about revisiting and healing her relationship with her parents—but perhaps not.

Denzel, however, was a different story. He smoked a great deal of marijuana on a regular basis. Although Bruce thought that they could do some useful work together, he believed that the work would be quite limited if Denzel didn't deal with his drug use. Bruce made it clear that they needed to address his use sooner rather than later; Denzel was free to disagree, but eventually they would have to stop therapy if he didn't accept this goal.

Goals Sometimes Change

As Polly's and Denzel's stories suggest, your goals for what you want to accomplish might change as you go along. Your initial goal may be to decide whether to stay in a relationship—but you may discover later that you also want to change some underlying patterns in your life that got you into the relationship in the first place. It's possible that your therapist will suggest goals that, at first, don't make sense to you—but later do. Conversely, as your therapy progresses, your therapist may reconsider goals that she at first thought were important.

Goals are good benchmarks. At any point, you and your therapist can revisit your goals to see whether you're on the track you said you'd be on. You may conclude that you're successfully moving along. On the other hand, you may decide that you aren't. If that's the case, you and your therapist can try to identify why things aren't working and what the two of you need to do about it.

An important aspect of the assessment and goal-setting process is that it sets the stage for the work of therapy. It helps ensure that you and your therapist understand and agree with each other about why you're there and what you are going to do. Without this understanding and agreement, you won't be able to do your therapeutic work.

CHAPTER 5

What Did You Mean By That?

Understanding How You and Your Therapist Talk to Each Other

Shared meaning is a communication term that means that the message sent is the message received. In psychotherapy, shared meaning also means mutual understanding and, ideally, mutual agreement regarding many aspects of the therapeutic relationship. Establishing shared meaning, developing trust, and handling issues related to power form the basis of a successful relationship between a therapist and a client.[1] In this chapter we focus on shared meaning. Later chapters will address issues of trust and power.

We have already looked at two ways that you and your therapist need to establish shared meaning: The first is making sure that you are clear about what to expect with regard to concrete matters such as cost, payment processes, and when and where you will meet for your sessions. The second is the treatment planning process. Here we'll consider more complex aspects of achieving shared meaning by examining the issues that may appear when you first meet your therapist and those that may continue throughout your work together.

Because therapy is a conversation, how we talk to each other is key to establishing shared meaning. What we intend to say is often not what the person on the receiving end hears. Sometimes it takes great effort to ensure that our messages are clearly understood.

There are many reasons why we misunderstand each other so often. One is simply our use of language itself. The greater the difference in two people's cultural background, the greater the difference in meaning we attribute to particular words, phrases, and tone of voice. *Crosstalk*, a video based on the work of sociolinguist John Gumperz,[2] demonstrates the cultural dimension of tone of voice and the ways in which inflection affects meaning. The tape shows two men at a bank in London making the same transaction, using the exact same script. One is British, the other Pakistani. The British man's sentences end on an up note, whereas the Pakistani man's end on a down note. It would be easy for some viewers to interpret the British man's statement as tentative and questioning and the Pakistani man's as demanding, but in fact both simply want to complete the transaction and move on. Our interpretation of someone's intention, whether because of simple inflection or some other cue that we interpret (or misinterpret), can have a big impact on our feelings about that person, and can create misunderstandings that may be difficult to repair.

My friends and family like to call me Twenty Questions Tamara because of my incurable curiosity about people, which is one of the reasons I became a therapist. I ask clients many questions to help us both get a better understanding of what's happening for them. "What do you think was behind your decision to do that?" "Can you tell me more about how you felt when I told you what I observed last week?" "What does 'bad' mean to you?" "What makes you assume that he meant to hurt you?" "How do you think this connects to what we talked about a few weeks ago?" Often this technique is very effective—but sometimes clients misunderstand. For example, I was helping my client Al explore what he thought had led him to withdraw during a disagreement with his sister. I did this by asking lots of probing questions. Al became very angry, insisting that he didn't know the answers to my questions. So I (of course) asked him what was making him angry with me. Al told me that he thought I expected certain answers from him; I was like a teacher who asked the class questions to which there was one right answer. He felt I was testing him to see if he knew the right answers. He was surprised and relieved to learn that I didn't know what he'd say, and didn't think there were right answers to my questions, but was working with him to discover *his* answers. "Sometimes I do have an idea of what the answer might be," I told him. "When that happens," I promised, "I'll let you know what I'm thinking. You won't have to guess. And my answer could be wrong. It will only be my best guess about what might be going on for you. I hope you'll let me know what doesn't seem right about it. That will help us both figure out what your right answer is."

Learning to understand what the other person is trying to say is central to any relationship. Although your therapist will be alert to whether the two of you are understanding one another, it's also important that you feel free to tell him how *you* interpret what he's saying and to tell him if you think he is not hearing you, so that you and he can clarify any misunderstandings.

Shared Styles

Style includes things such as whether your therapist has a sense of humor you enjoy; whether she's direct or tactful in how she says things; whether she talks a lot or very little; whether she sets a clear agenda and covers topics in a specific order during the session or whether you can talk about whatever is on your mind; and whether her office setting is formal or casual.

Before meeting with a client, Nancy, a therapist, sends him or her a long intake form to fill out and bring to the first session. She works in a clinic, so many clients sit in a big waiting room and are called up for their appointments by the receptionist. Nancy's office itself has stiff, upright chairs, a big desk, a few pictures and, most prominently, a slew of academic degrees on the wall. Upon first meeting a client, she introduces herself as Dr. Allen. This isn't done for effect; it's who Nancy is. When Georgie, a potential client, had her first appointment with Nancy, she thought Nancy was impersonal and cold. So she didn't come back and instead began working with Janna, whose casual demeanor and home office, filled with children's toys, pictures of her family, and comfortable furniture, felt warm and inviting to her. Yet, Georgie's cousin Terrie considered Nancy's professional stance far more credible and trustworthy than Janna's casual approach.

Or consider Glen, who considers his therapist's no-nonsense comments a breath of fresh air. He recommended the therapist to his friend Carl, but to Carl, the same therapist's approach felt critical and shaming.

The style question is more important than it might seem. You want a therapist whose style puts you at ease. Also, like so much in the therapeutic relationship, how you respond to your therapist's style says at least as much about you as about her. Maybe Nancy reminded Georgie of someone who had treated her badly and, had she been able to get past her initial discomfort, she could have revised her initial ideas about what to expect from "that type of person." Perhaps Georgie preferred Janna's style because, like most people, she was comfortable with what she found familiar. Janna's looser boundaries may have reminded Georgie of those in her family, which, she would later discover, were sometimes loose to a damaging degree.

"DO YOU UNDERSTAND WHAT IT'S LIKE TO BE ME?"

For you to feel safe with your therapist, it's extremely important that he understands you and your life experience. We all need to be deeply known. People who know us deeply don't have to agree with us all the time. However, it is important that they understand how we perceive our experience and how we arrived at our perceptions. We experience this knowing as compassion.

A goal of therapy is for you to gain more self-awareness— to understand what it's like to be you, how you perceive things, and how you got to where you are right now. If I'm doing my job well, my reflecting back to people what they say in my own words—not just repeating theirs—has several effects. First, they experience me as genuinely wanting to understand them. This alone is important. Second, if I get it right, they have the very profound experience of being known, which then helps them move toward greater clarity. Often we are confused or vague about what we're really thinking or feeling, and we could use some help in seeing our thoughts and emotions more clearly. I can serve as a mirror for my clients. They can look in the mirror and see whether what I am saying really reflects what they are trying to articulate. We work together to arrive at a shared understanding of what they are trying to say and what it means to them.

My client Lynette had an interaction with her boss that upset her, but she wasn't quite sure why. He asked her to do a task that she was quite capable of doing, but something about it didn't feel right. In our conversation, I asked her to expand a bit on "didn't feel right."

Lynette: I don't really know how to say it. I just felt a lot of pressure about the job he asked me to do.

Tamara: Pressure to . . . ?

Lynette: Do it right. It was really important that I do it right. But it's weird. Because the task wasn't that hard, I really didn't think I'd have a problem with it.

Tamara: Was there something about how he asked you that put pressure on you?

Lynette: Hmmm. Well . . . he did seem kind of anxious. . . .

Tamara: How do you think his anxiety put pressure on you?

Lynette: I don't know. I just started to feel nervous, too.

Tamara: Maybe you felt the need to take care of him in some way.

Lynette: Yes, that's it. I felt like if I didn't do this right, he would look bad.

Tamara: And it was your job to prevent that? Or to make him look good?

Lynette: Yes.

Tamara: What if you didn't ?

Lynette: I'm not sure. I don't believe he'd fire me.

Tamara: But it does seem as if you're afraid there could be a pretty bad consequence.

Lynette: Yeah, it feels that way. He wouldn't respect me as much.

Tamara: It sounds like you're saying that in order to deserve his esteem, you have to make him look good in others' eyes. Your work, by itself, isn't enough.

Lynette: Uh-huh, I think that's it. Now that I think of it, I often feel like it's my duty to make others look good—and if I don't, they won't see me as worth much. It happens at work all the time, and sometimes it happens at home too, like when my son asks me for something, I feel like I have to give him what he wants or he'll be angry with me and reject me.

We're all different in terms of what makes us feel that others understand us. Here are some statements from a variety of people, all clients, describing how they knew their therapists understood them.[3]

- "He said exactly what I had felt."
- "I thought I saw her eyes water, and I had the impression that she truly understood and felt entirely what I was experiencing."
- "I described my feelings, and I felt that she felt what I was telling her."
- "I [said] it wasn't easy to live with one's parents. . . . He then indicated that at [my age] . . . he too had to settle things with his parents. . . . I wasn't the only one in this situation."
- "The therapist had seen into me, had [seen] the hidden sense of my thought."
- "I find my [therapist] extremely attentive . . . [she's] extremely present."

"HAVE YOU WALKED IN MY SHOES?"

Many clients want to know whether their therapist shares a similar life experience. Sometimes a client believes that only a woman, an African-American, a lesbian, or someone who has struggled with her particular issue (for example, substance abuse, incest, or anxiety) can really understand what it's like to walk in her shoes. It may be necessary for someone to have lived your own experience to really get who you are and how your feel. Or it may not be necessary at all. It all depends on the individual client and therapist.

Jovita said she would never have gone to therapy had she not met Shirley, her African-American therapist. She didn't believe therapy was for people like her. It was only for rich white people. She was surprised that an African-American woman was even in the profession. She didn't believe a white therapist could possibly understand some of the issues she faced. For example, how could a white person understand why she believed her stepfather sexually abused her because she had very dark skin?

But it turned out that Shirley didn't understand Jovita very well after all. She made assumptions about Jovita that were inaccurate, and she seemed unable to hear Jovita's attempts at clarification. So Jovita looked for someone else and found an Asian-American therapist who understood her deeply. She learned that her therapist did not need to have her exact experience. But had she not met Shirley, Jovita never would have gotten in the door. And, Jovita did need a therapist who understood what it was like for her to be African-American. Later she worked with a white therapist, but, in her words, "I tested her first" to make sure that she could truly empathize with a woman of color.

Axel, who was beginning to acknowledge that he was gay, felt it important to see a gay therapist who could understand, from the inside, what he was going through. Later, when he was more confident about his identity, his therapist's sexual orientation was no longer important to him. He did effective work with a straight man, who understood his challenges very well.

THE ADVANTAGES AND DISADVANTAGES OF INSIDE EMPATHY: "DOES IT REALLY MEAN YOU UNDERSTAND ME?"

I know things about being a parent that I couldn't possibly have understood in the same way had I not had children. In fact, I could say that about every aspect of my personal experience, from being a woman, to being a teacher, to having curly hair, to being Jewish, to having divorced and remarried, and so on. This phenomenon, which I call *inside empathy*, can enhance your relationship with your therapist.

Marie, a writer, appreciated her therapist's love for and astute understanding of literature. Eileen and her therapist connected around their mutual love of rock climbing. Saul liked knowing that he and his therapist watched many of the same movies and TV shows and shared an interest in basketball. All of these things can help us feel more connected to our therapists because we know that they understand something about our world.

However, there's another side to this equation. It's easy but inaccurate to assume that because your therapist is like you in some way, he had the same experiences you had and sees them the way you do. My experience as a parent is *my* experience, not yours. It could be similar to yours in many ways, but you have different children, a different family constellation, and a different history. You may be disappointed, hurt, or angry when my take on things is not what you expect, given our shared experience. In addition, some people end up comparing themselves to their therapists in ways that are neither accurate nor useful. Both Ben and his therapist Aaron were recovering alcoholics. Ben assumed that, unlike himself, Aaron never struggled to maintain sobriety. He could have used this assumption to generate hope: "If Aaron can do it, so can I." Or he could have put himself down, seeing himself as a failure for not achieving what he imagines Aaron has.

The other danger of overvaluing inside empathy is that you might discount what your therapist has to offer just because she *hasn't* had your experience. In doing so, you risk missing the opportunity to learn something important about yourself.

Dave knew that his therapist, Jane, had been married for a long time and had children and grandchildren. In contrast, Dave was divorced and his children lived with their mother. Although he made attempts to stay connected with them, he felt constantly sabotaged by his ex-wife, who too often found last-minute reasons why the children couldn't spend time with him. Furthermore, she did not inform him of meetings with teachers and other events in their lives, leaving him in the dark. Over time, he began to see his ex-wife's attitude toward him rubbing off on their children. When they did visit him, they called their mother frequently, or she called them. He believed that neither they nor their mother felt the children were completely safe with him, and he was angry with all of them. Furthermore, they seemed to reject any attempt he made to show them a different picture of who he was. The harder he tried, the more distant they became.

Dave felt a lot of pain about being sidelined as a father. He felt victimized by his ex-wife and railed against the injustice of his situation to anyone who would listen.

Jane felt a lot of compassion for Dave but also noted in a session that his attachment to feeling and behaving like a victim created more pain for him and further deepened the rift between himself and his children. Dave rejected this feedback. He couldn't get past the idea that Jane, a woman who had never experienced divorce, didn't understand how impossible his ex-wife made it for him have any other reaction. Nor could she possibly understand the ways in which the courts favored women in divorce cases, further victimizing men. When Jane suggested that he gave his ex-wife and the system too much power to orchestrate both how he viewed his situation and how he behaved, Dave insisted that she would react the same way, were she in his situation.

At the same time that Jane communicated a great deal of compassion for his painful circumstances and sense of powerlessness, she continued to encourage Dave to examine his victim stance. It perpetuated his pain and aggravated the tension between him and his children. Eventually, he began to accept some responsibility. Yes, his ex and children were unfair. Yes, his therapist would probably react the same way in the situation. Yes, anyone might. The issue wasn't whether he had good reason for how he felt, but whether his attachment to being a victim was serving him and his children well. At last he realized that discrediting Jane because she hadn't walked in his shoes enabled him to avoid facing the consequences of his own victim stance more squarely.

Of course, there may be very good reasons for choosing a therapist based on his or her similar life experience. If you have a history of being abused by men, you may need to see a female therapist to feel safe enough to open your heart. If you have experienced discrimination or abuse from white people, you may need a person of color, as Jovita did, simply to walk through the door.

However, it's equally possible that working with the very type of person who abused you will help heal a wound. Although working with a woman might feel initially safer, more familiar, and more comfortable, working with a man could force you to deal with your fears about men more directly, as you encounter the same feelings in your relationship with your therapist. Working with a man could also give you an opportunity to experience a different outcome.

For some clients, the last person they want to work with is someone like themsleves. Arielle chose her therapist precisely because she did *not* have the same religious background. Arielle was concerned that someone who shared her conservative upbringing would disapprove of the way she felt about her religion and how she was choosing to live her life. Lonnie wanted a male therapist who was older than he, because, Lonnie assumed, he would know more about life and have a wider perspective on it than Lonnie did.

Some aspects of your therapist's personal experience are obvious, but most are not. Your therapist may or may not be willing to talk with you about his own beliefs and life experience. If your therapist asks you to explore why you want to know whether he's a Christian, divorced, alcoholic, or a parent—rather than simply answering the question— he's not being evasive or secretive. He's asking because he knows that your question has meaning for you.

The meaning is what counts. What would it mean for you to know I'm Jewish too? What would it mean if I'm not? How would it affect your ability to find what I have to offer useful? Are you concerned that I won't be able to understand you or help you? If you found out that, yes, I'm married, would you feel bad about yourself or compare yourself negatively (or positively) to me because you're not? If you found out I've been divorced, would you worry that I'd push you to make the same decision rather than help you figure out how to stay in your marriage?

Most clients with whom I have discussed this issue conclude that these types of external characteristics are not important so long as their therapist is able to really understand and help them. However, if you believe you need someone who defines herself in a particular way, your feelings about this are important. Understanding how you came to them will help you learn something about yourself.

When my colleague, Aziza, who is Somali, first started work as a therapist, she noticed that she treated those from her community differently than those from mainstream America. Her sessions would be less structured and more informal, more like they would be had they sought her advice as an elder in the community. She was concerned that if she went into too much detail about assessment and treatment planning, the way she did with her non-Somali clients, they would find it unfamiliar and intimidating. When people visit the elder, they just want to talk about what's on their minds or to seek advice about what to do. They don't set goals. They don't follow the same protocols for confidentiality. If they met the elder in another context, they would certainly acknowledge each other and might even continue the conversation they'd had when they sought advice. She didn't breach her ethical obligation about confidentiality, but she worried that her clients wouldn't understand such seemingly artificial barriers.

Aziza came to realize that her less formal approach was actually confusing to her clients, some of whom found it patronizing and unprofessional. She came up with a way to resolve her role confusion and resulting loss of shared meaning. Now she volunteers at her church, where she plays the elder role the way that role should be played. But if someone seeks her help as a therapist, she is consistent in her approach to that role no matter what ethnic or national background her client has.

It still matters to some of her Somali clients that Aziza is herself Somali and understands their culture from the inside. However, when she's in the role of therapist, she plays a mainstream role that, in Aziza's opinion, should not be compromised. Now people know what to expect depending on where they talk with her.

Achieving shared meaning with your therapist will enable you to have a more productive experience in therapy. You will feel that you are both "on board" in your mutual project to enhance your growth. The more you feel this way, the more you will trust your therapist.

So far, I've discussed those aspects of therapy that are common to all therapeutic approaches. However, each therapist does have a particular approach and a set of strategies he or she uses to work with you. Another important aspect of shared meaning is whether your therapist's approach to the work makes sense to you—that is, do you understand what he's doing and agree that it's helpful? The next two chapters promise you some basic information to help you understand what your therapist is doing and why.

CHAPTER 6

Approaches to Therapy

In our discussion of the common factors shared in any type of therapy, I mentioned that there are hundreds of approaches to therapy. Some approaches are broadly useful and some have been developed to address particular issues or problems. All of them are ways of understanding and explaining what makes people tick and what helps them change, and all of them are ways of providing the necessary ingredients for change described in Chapters Two and Three.

Many therapists draw from multiple approaches, even in their work with one client. Others see things through one particular theoretical lens. Your therapist may or may not specifically discuss the theory or theories behind the approach he is taking, although he'll probably tell you if you ask him. However, the way he talks to you, the kinds of things he asks you about, and the ideas he has for what you can do in and between sessions are all reflections of how he thinks about therapy and about life in general. Again, what's important is not so much which approach he uses as whether it feels right and makes sense to you.

In this chapter I describe four major theoretical approaches to therapy: psychodynamic, cognitive–behavioral, humanistic, and family systems. Most of the different therapeutic approaches are variations of one or more of these four. And, although each of the four approaches has different emphases and assumptions, there is a great deal of overlap among them.

To help you understand the approaches, we'll take one couple, Rose and Ernesto Diaz, and look at how their therapist José worked with them, drawing ideas from each approach. Ernesto and Rose came to therapy because, as parents, they were concerned about their 13-year-old son Alberto, whose behavior at school was troubling. Teachers reported that he bullied other kids and was disrespectful to those in authority. He was also beginning to argue loudly with his father. The couple has been married for 15 years, and they have two younger children, Tia, 11, and Fredrik, 9, neither of whom worry them at this point. Ernesto's parents are from Mexico and moved to the United States when Ernesto was 3 years old. Rose's parents are of Finnish descent; her grandparents immigrated to the United States in the early 1900s.

THE PSYCHODYNAMIC APPROACH

Sigmund Freud, often called the father of psychotherapy, was the first to develop the theory behind psychoanalytic or psychodynamic therapy. In the last hundred years, many therapists and scholars have revised and expanded upon

Freud's initial ideas.[1] Although each contribution to psychodynamic theory is unique, all share several features:

- A belief in the importance of the unconscious
- An emphasis on stages of personal development
- A perspective that assumes that personal history shapes
  people's present circumstances
- A process of working through issues and concerns
- A belief in the centrality of the therapeutic relationship.

FOCUS ON THE UNCONSCIOUS

The first premise of psychodynamic theory is that it is important to identify and explore people's unconscious processes.
Psychodynamic thinkers assume that our conscious responses
to ourselves and the world do not include awareness of the
strong, and often painful, emotions stored in the limbic brain
that may underlie or drive those responses. Related to this
concept is the idea of defenses: those strategies we develop to
avoid thoughts and feelings that seem too overwhelming or
anxiety-provoking to face. Interpretation—suggesting underlying explanations for how a client is responding—is a common technique in psychodynamic therapy that aims to bring
the unconscious to light. The purpose of making the unconscious conscious is to change old unproductive patterns and
behaviors in order to make the client's life and social relationships richer and more satisfying. Although this is a key aspect
of the psychodynamic approach, it's not something a therapist
typically attempts until the client is ready to tolerate those
emotions that he is trying to avoid.

The following conversation involving José and Ernesto
and Rose took place after the first several meetings.

Ernesto: She agrees with me when we decide on a punishment for Alberto, but then she lets him off the hook!

José: That must be frustrating.

Ernesto: It sure is!

José: Have you ever asked her why she changes her mind?

Ernesto: She says she didn't. Or she gives some reason why he should really be able to do whatever it was we said he shouldn't do.

José: But the reason doesn't make sense to you?

Ernesto: Most of the time, no.

José: Rose, how do you see it?

Rose: I do agree with Ernesto, mostly. I don't like the way Alberto is behaving. And most times I think he ought to be punished. But not all the time.

José: Is it hard to talk about it with Ernesto when you *don't* think he should be punished?

Rose: I guess so.

José: What makes it hard?

Rose: He just seems so set. I guess I don't think I could convince him to change his mind.

José: Sounds like you decide it's not worth trying.

Rose: I suppose . . .

José: I've noticed sometimes in our conversations that when you and Ernesto start to disagree on something, you tend to just get quiet, or you change your mind and agree with him. Is that what happens at home too?

Rose: Yes . . . sometimes. . . .

José: Can you describe, from your point of view, what happens?

Rose: He gets mad. And I don't feel like he really listens to me, anyway. I just go into another room. Like I said, he doesn't really listen. And he shouts. I don't like that.

José: Does it seem easier, then, just to avoid disagreements than to risk that?

Rose: In some ways.

After further discussing Rose's reluctance to risk Ernesto's anger by expressing a differing point of view, José offered the following observation:

José: I hear you telling me that it's difficult for you to disagree with your husband and to support him when he disciplines your son, so I wonder if there's a part of you that kind of admires Alberto's ability to stand up to his father. Do you think that's possible?

This observation is an example of interpretation. By raising this possibility, José opened the door to explore whether Rose unconsciously encouraged Alberto to argue with his father, perhaps because she was afraid to do so herself. This might explain her overt agreement with Ernesto and her covert support of Alberto, which she expressed by not following through on the limits she and Ernesto had set with him.

Seeing People from a Developmental Perspective

According to psychodynamic theory, people must move through each phase of life successfully to go on to the next. These phases are not completely linear, nor are they separate from one another. (An example of a developmental scheme is the one proposed by Erik Erickson,[2] part of which I discuss in Chapter Ten.) People revisit developmental issues from earlier phases when they enter new ones. However, people can get stuck at a certain point of development and can use the therapy relationship as a way to resolve and move through them.

Related to the idea of development is the assumption that we are shaped by our histories and that we recreate the past in the present. Accordingly, we are likely to be in relationships that reflect our histories—or at least our stories about what those histories were. We choose people as friends and partners who are, in some way, like the people we have known before, and we tend to react to people in the present as if they were like people in our past.

José observed that Ernesto seemed insecure in his role as Alberto's father. Whenever Alberto misbehaved, Ernesto would respond with angry and harsh criticism. When Rose didn't back him up, he became angry with her. José initiated the following conversation:

José: Ernesto, all of us parents learned from our own parents something about how to raise kids. I think it helps to understand something about our own experience as kids. Could you describe a bit of what you learned from your parents?

Ernesto: My father was real critical of me.

José: How did he let you know that?

Ernesto: One thing I remember is how he'd blow up when I couldn't do my homework. He'd start yelling.

José: Do you remember how you felt at those times?

Ernesto: Really bad. Scared.

José: Were you worried he'd hit you or anything?

Ernesto: No. He'd just blow up. Scream. Yell that I'd never amount to anything. But I never got in trouble, like with drinking and all that. But I just never seemed to be able to do what I was supposed to do. Not well enough, anyway.

José: That sounds painful. It must have been confusing.

Ernesto: Yeah, I worried. I felt like I was no good, but I didn't know why.

José: Those feelings can stay with people. What did you do with that?

Ernesto: Yeah, I think I still feel that way sometimes. It stuck with me.

José: I'm curious—what did your mother do when your father would yell at you like that?

Ernesto: Nothing. She'd just sit there. Once in a while she'd come into my room later and give me a hug, or a piece of cake, or something. But she never said anything. And lots of times she'd just sit there while he was screaming and then go do something else.

José: What was that like for you?

Ernesto: I always knew Mama loved me. But sometimes I wished she'd say that Papa was wrong. She never did.

José: What did you think was going on with her?

Ernesto: I don't know. She never said . . . I guess maybe I just believed Papa was right that I was no good.

José: When your wife doesn't back you up, I wonder if it feels like she is criticizing you, like your father, or not supporting you, like your mother.

Ernesto: Well, yeah. Both of those.

José: I can imagine that, when Rose doesn't support you, it could make you feel pretty bad—like you did when you were a kid.

Ernesto: She leaves me there alone. Like she told you. She even walks out—goes to another room, kind of like my mother did, when my father would yell at me.

Later in the conversation, José asked Ernesto how he felt when Alberto treated him disrespectfully.

Ernesto: I get really mad.

José: What do you say to yourself?

Ernesto: He doesn't respect me like he should.

José: Can you say more about what it means that he doesn't respect you?

Ernesto: He treats me like I'm nothing. I'm his father. I've done a lot for him. I help him out, go to his school events, work hard so he can have what he needs. And now he just treats me like some no-good neighbor. A kid who respected his father wouldn't do that.

José: It sounds like you're doing everything you can to be a good father to him. You know, I'm thinking that when Alberto challenges you, maybe it reminds you of how your dad treated you. You told me your son treats you like you're nothing. This sounds like what you told me about your dad. Feeling similar to the way you did when you were a kid could make being a father difficult. What do you think?

Ernesto: That could be. Sometimes I just feel like a loser.

As they talked further, it emerged that Ernesto's father's rage was exacerbated by his father's belief that, as a Mexican-American, his son would need to prove himself in the face of discrimination and his fear that his son would fail to do so. Although his father's criticism was meant to protect Ernesto by pushing him to perform better, Ernesto responded by feeling completely inadequate—a feeling further reinforced by his mother's failure to support him.

Today, Ernesto reacted to any challenge or perceived challenge, even that from his teenage son, with the same shame he'd felt as a child. To come to terms with his son and his wife, he would have to step beyond his own difficult history with his parents.

WORKING THROUGH

The expression *working through* refers to the idea that after we have an insight, or understanding, we go through a process of reaching emotional resolution and changing our behaviors. We come at the issue again and again from different angles. This process allows us to integrate it, not just intellectually, but emotionally and physically as well. In the language of brain science, we connect the neuro-networks related to cognition—the key insight—with those related to emotions and behaviors.

Ernesto began to understand himself better because of conversations like the ones shown here. As he continued in therapy, he worked on his shame and feelings of inadequacy as they emerged in different areas of his life—at work, in other interactions with Rose, and sometimes with his friends. In time, his feelings about himself began to shift.

USE OF THE THERAPEUTIC RELATIONSHIP

For all psychodynamic approaches, the relationship between therapist and client is not only essential, as it is in all therapies, but is a major focus of the treatment. A psychodynamic therapist will draw explicit attention to what is happening between her and her client and what it means. Because of the tendency to recreate the past, we are likely to replay our history in the therapy relationship as well. Psychodynamic therapists call this phenomenon *transference*. The way a client perceives and treats a therapist provides clues that both therapist and client can use to understand how the client perceives and treats others, and how this may reflect the past more than the current situation. This process can pave the way for a corrective experience wherein the client has the chance to experience a new kind of relationship—one that helps to heal old wounds and to encourage growth.

We saw an example of transference and the corrective experience in the conversation between Rachel and Bob in Chapter Two. Recall that Rachel didn't expect Bob to be able to help her and unconsciously attempted to push him away. Instead, Bob stuck with her, communicating that he could and wanted to help her and that she deserved to have his help.

Here, we see an example of this dynamic in an interaction between Ernesto and José.

José: I've noticed that sometimes when I say something about Alberto, you
          bristle a bit. Have you noticed that, too?

Ernesto: Uh-huh. Sometimes.

José: Could you tell me what bothers you?

Ernesto: I don't know. I think you don't really understand what it's like to
          be a parent.

José: What gives you that feeling?

Ernesto: You act like he's a bad kid.

José: Really! Can you tell me more about what I say that gives you that im-
          pression?

Ernesto: When you say things like he's testing the limits.

José: And that sounds like I'm saying he's a bad kid?

Ernesto: Yeah, or that I'm a bad parent. Like I said before, a kid should re-
          spect his parents. And obviously Alberto isn't doing that. Espe-
          cially not with me.

José: You hear me criticizing him—and criticizing you, too. That's inter-
          esting, because I thought I was just describing and rewording what
          you were telling me. Actually, I'm impressed with your parenting
          and your commitment to your son. What's it like to hear me say
          this?

Ernesto: I'm surprised. I didn't think you respected me at all.

José: You know, it sounds like you almost expected me to criticize you. Do
          you think that might be true?

Ernesto: Maybe. After all, Alberto's been in trouble at school. The teach-
          ers are always calling to complain.

José: It always feels bad when someone criticizes your kid. Even if your kid
          is acting up! Alberto's obviously had some struggles recently. I won-
          der if you also expected me to be critical because of what we've
          talked about before—you know, about the way your father criticized
          you when you were young. That kind of thing often sets us up to ex-
          pect the same reaction from others. It can make it difficult to believe
          someone's really in your corner.

Ernesto: It's not just my father. I've gotten it from my boss, too. I'm always looking over my shoulder.

José: I'm thinking also about when we've talked about being Mexican— that feeling that you have to prove yourself. Do you suppose that adds to your expectations about how others will see you? You seem to have gotten a double whammy: parental criticism and the culture's criticism of Mexicans.

Ernesto: I think about it all the time. I wonder sometimes if that's why Alberto gets in trouble at school. Maybe if he did the same kinds of things but wasn't Mexican, the teachers wouldn't be so hard on him.

José: Could be. But when you worry about that, how does it affect the way you react to Alberto?

Ernesto: I don't want that for him. I want him to straighten up. I don't want him to suffer.

José: So you get harder on him partly because you want to protect him from being treated unfairly?

Ernesto: Something like that.

José: Do you think your father felt that way, too?

Ernesto: Maybe so.

José: So, now, here I am, another Mexican man. It's not hard to imagine you might think I'm going to do the same thing. What's it like to have me react differently?

Ernesto: I'm going to have to think about it. I think it feels good. It's hard to believe.

THE DIFFERENCE BETWEEN PSYCHOANALYSIS AND PSYCHODYNAMIC THERAPY

The terms *psychoanalytic* and *psychodynamic* describe a similar way of thinking about and approaching clients. Both adhere to the concepts described above. However, psychoanalysis usually lasts a very long time; sessions are often several times a week for several years; and the client is encouraged to talk about whatever comes to mind. There is no specific agenda or format for the session. Psychodynamic therapy can be much shorter, even as short as a few months; the sessions are less frequent—one or sometimes two times a week; and the therapist is more active and more directive—for example, keeping the client more focused on resolving a particular issue.

THE COGNITIVE–BEHAVIORAL APPROACH

The other day I saw a bumper sticker on the car in front of me, offering a useful reminder: *Don't believe everything you think.* This is the premise of cognitive theory: that our experience of life is based not so much on the objective situation we are in, as on our thoughts about it. Unlike psychodynamic thinkers, who often regard strong emotion as shaping our thinking and behavior, early cognitive theorists regarded our thinking as shaping emotion and behavior. Early behavior theorists assumed that all behavior could be traced to stimuli in the immediate environment that either reinforced or diminished particular ways of acting.[3]

Few therapists today believe that one can shape behavior by focusing solely on either the cognitive or the behavioral aspects of human experience, especially when working with adults. Cognitive–behavioral therapy (CBT), developed by more recent theorists,[4] focuses on the interaction between thinking and behavior, and the effect of both on feelings. Although cognitive–behavioral therapists emphasize the thinking part of the equation, they intervene on both cognitive and behavioral levels. Major aspects of this approach include a focus on multiple levels of thinking, the use of a great deal of structure and specific techniques, and little direct focus on the therapeutic relationship itself.

LEVELS OF THINKING

Automatic thoughts, intermediate thoughts, and core beliefs are different levels of thinking about ourselves and the world. Cognitive–behaviorists seek to help clients identify and modify their thinking on all three levels. Automatic thoughts are those fleeting thoughts that rise up immediately when we're faced with a situation. Sometimes instead of thoughts, we just see a picture—for example, someone glaring at us. We have automatic thoughts all the time, but the therapist is interested in the *hot* ones—the ones with strong emotional charge. Beneath automatic thoughts are core beliefs about ourselves and the world. Positive core beliefs include "I'm reliable and trustworthy" and "There's a place for me in the world." Examples of negative core beliefs are "I'm a bad person" and "I'm stupid."

Intermediate thoughts consist of values and assumptions as well as strategies that people develop to cope with their beliefs. For example, someone who believes he's stupid might have a value that "only really smart, knowledgeable people are worthy of respect." He might further assume, "If I don't say what's on my mind, others won't know how stupid I am." The accompanying strategies might be "Never ask a question in public" or "Never express a point of view on something where you don't have all the facts."

Using this approach, José helped both Rose and Ernesto identify their automatic thoughts, intermediate thoughts, and core beliefs in reaction to Alberto's teacher's complaints about their son.

José: Rose, when you got the phone call from the teacher, what was the first thing that went through your mind?

Rose: Uh-oh!

José: Uh-oh, what? Did you have any thoughts after that?

Rose: Here we go again.

José: So it was familiar to you. What seemed familiar?

Rose: I'm in trouble again.

José: So, the teacher calls about Alberto, and it sounds like your first thoughts are about *your* having done something wrong and that you're in trouble. Is that what you're saying?

Rose: Yes.

José: Let's explore that some more. How are you in trouble?

Rose: The teacher's mad. Ernesto's going to be mad.

José: And what will happen then?

Rose: They'll think badly of me.

José: What kinds of things will they think?

Rose: I messed up. I didn't get Alberto to behave right.

José: What does that mean, if you didn't do that?

Rose: I'm a bad mother.

José: So if you were a good mother, you could get Alberto to behave right?

Rose: Yes. I'd keep him in line.

José: Thinking you're a bad mother is painful enough. I'm wondering if there are other thoughts that go with that? What does it mean about you if you're a bad mother?

Rose: I'm a failure—a bad person.

José: How much do you believe that you're a failure or a bad person, say, on a scale of 1–100, with 100 being all the time?

Rose: I'd say at least 96.

José: Wow. Do you have any evidence that you might not be a complete failure?

Rose: Not that I can think of at the moment.

José: What do you say, for instance, about the fact that you're doing well at work?

Rose: Well, I guess I do okay there, but work isn't nearly as important as doing a good job as a mother. And besides, I'm not anything special.

José: So, it sounds like to be less than a failure, you not only have to do okay, you have to be special.

Rose: Yes.

Rose's automatic thoughts were "uh-oh" and "here we go again." Her intermediate thoughts included three important if–then contingencies: (1) If she kept Alberto in line and got him to behave right, then she'd be a good mother; (2) if she stayed out of trouble, people wouldn't be mad at her and think badly of her; and (3) if she was special, then she wouldn't be a failure. At the core is her belief that she's bad—a failure.

A similar process with Ernesto revealed a remarkably parallel set of beliefs. This was helpful for both Ernesto and Rose, as they could see that, although they often felt at odds with each other, they shared beliefs that caused them pain, both as individuals and as a couple.

CBT focuses on those automatic thoughts, intermediate thoughts, and core beliefs that involve *dysfunctional thinking,* that is, that lead to problems. Examples include all-or-nothing thinking ("I'm always in trouble; she never listens"); catastrophizing ("If I make a mistake, I'll lose my job"); emotional reasoning ("I'm terrified of the dark, so it must be dangerous"); and mind reading ("He didn't ask my opinion because he thinks I'm incompetent").

THE THERAPEUTIC PROCESS

In their purest form, CBT sessions follow a predictable format. The elements of each session include:

- Getting an update from the client on how things are going for him or her.
- Checking the client's mood, perhaps using a quick test designed to rate, for example, the level of the client's depression.
- Discussing what the client thought of the previous session—for example, what the client felt was helpful.
- Setting the agenda for the day's session by listing the topics the client would like to address, and deciding what the client thinks is most important to begin with.
- Reviewing the previous week's homework assignment.
- Discussing the issues on the agenda.
- Discussing what homework assignments the client will work on before the following meeting.

CBT is usually short term, lasting perhaps 6–12 sessions. Clients are expected to identify the problem and how they would like it to be different. Therapists help them identify specific goals that can be measured in behavioral terms. Although exploration of the past is part of the process because we form core beliefs early in life, the main focus is on the client's current thinking and on ways to modify it when it isn't working well.

CBT therapists educate clients about the principles of the theory, including how their thinking affects such conditions as depression and anxiety. They also use many techniques that help people identify, challenge, and modify their dysfunctional thoughts. This process is called *cognitive restructuring.* For example, the therapist might engage in Socratic questioning, challenging the client to evaluate the validity of his or her views. For Rose, such a conversation looked like this:

José: You're saying that you're a bad mother because Alberto is having trouble at school, right?

Rose: Yes.

José: Let's look at your belief about being a bad mother for a minute, okay?

Rose: Okay.

José: That seems like a pretty big statement, based on the fact that one of your kids is struggling right now. What's happening with the other two?

Rose: Well . . . They're doing fine, I guess. Tia was having trouble in school for a while, but we straightened it out.

José: You did? How did you do that?

Rose: She was getting in fights on the bus with other girls. We talked about other ways she could handle it if she was upset. She came up with a plan to talk to the bus driver and to move her seat away from those kids.

José: What do you make of that?

Rose: I guess she's pretty good at figuring things out.

José: Well, that's interesting. You blame yourself when one kid is in trouble but give your kid all the credit when things work out. Did you notice that?

Rose: Not till you said it.

José: Could it possibly be that you had something to do with helping Tia out?

Rose: I guess so. Sure. Yes.

José: What would that do to your conclusion that you're a bad mother?

Rose: Well, I guess it's not always true.

José: Let's take it a little further. What if Tia had continued to have trouble, and you asked me for help to figure out what to do about it?

Rose: If she continued to have trouble, I think I'd feel the way I do about Alberto.

José: So the fact that you were asking for help about him? What would you say about that?

Rose: That I obviously can't figure things out on my own.

José: And?

Rose: I must be pretty dumb.

José: That's interesting. I usually think it's a sign of intelligence to ask for help when you're not sure what to do. A sign that you've got some strength. Does that make sense?

Rose: I'm not sure.

José: Let's look at it this way. What if you knew two mothers whose kids were having a hard time and neither of them could figure out a way to help their kids? Who would you think was doing her best as a mother? The one who just let the problem go on and did nothing about it, or the one who asked for some help?

Rose: The one who asked for help.

José: Okay. So, you can see that asking for help with Alberto is actually an argument *against* your belief that you're a bad mother?

Rose: Yeah, I can see that.

In CBT, clients are assigned homework tasks. The belief is that the client has to practice identifying and challenging thoughts on a regular basis, not just once a week in a therapy session. Such practice strengthens the neural connections between cognitions and emotions, enabling the client to use her prefrontal cortex to modify the hot cognitions and the strong feelings that accompany them.[5] The tasks also give the client tools she can continue to use once therapy is over. A common task is to suggest that a client fill out "Thought Records"[6] like the one Rose created.

Table 6.1 Tracking, evaluating, and changing moods and automatic thoughts: Rose

SITUATION	MOODS	AUTOMATIC THOUGHTS (OR PICTURES)	EVIDENCE THAT SUPPORTS THE HOT THOUGHT	EVIDENCE THAT DOES NOT SUPPORT THE HOT THOUGHT	ALTERNATIVE/ BALANCED THOUGHTS	RATE MOODS NOW
Who? What? Where? When?	A. What did you feel? B. Rate the intensity of each mood. (1 = very mild and 100 = very strong)	A. What was going through your mind just before you started to feel this way? Any other thoughts? Images? B. Underline the hot thought(s).			Rate the degree to which you believe the alternative thought. (1–100)	Re-rate moods listed in column 2 as well as any new moods. (1–100)
Wednesday, 3:00 P.M., Alberto's teacher called and left a message that Alberto refused to cooperate in class.	Shame (90)	I can't get him to behave! The teacher must think I'm terrible. (hot thought) I'm a bad mother. (really hot thought)	She sounded irritated in her message. She's told me that Alberto really needs to change his behavior. Alberto doesn't do what I tell him to do.	Last time we spoke she told me how much she respected how hard I'm trying with Alberto. Yesterday and the day before, Alberto stopped watching TV and did his homework when I asked him to. All my kids talk to me when they're feeling bad about something.	The teacher cares about Alberto. She's calling because she's concerned. (80) Maybe the tone in her voice was because she was tired after a long day with the kids —not because she was upset with me or Alberto. (60) All kids ignore their parents sometimes. (90) I don't do everything right as a mother, but I always try my best. (90)	Shame (50) Confident (45)

Therapists generally use behavioral techniques to help clients experiment with different ways of acting—for example, practicing being more assertive, either in sessions or outside—and asking them to evaluate the outcome of each experiment, especially its impact on their initial thoughts and beliefs. Other behavioral techniques include systematic desensitization, in which clients visualize being exposed to increasingly anxiety-provoking situations while using relaxation techniques to calm down, thus retraining their bodies and becoming more able to manage the fear.

The Therapeutic Relationship

Although the relationship between client and therapist is important in CBT, it is not a focus of the sessions. Rather, the emphasis is on establishing a relationship in which both client and therapist collaborate on the goals and tasks of treatment. The only time the relationship might be a focus of attention is if the therapist uses the client's thoughts about the therapist or the therapy as an opportunity to practice the process of CBT. This can be particularly helpful if there is some problem in the client–therapist relationship that CBT could help resolve.

The Humanistic Approach

Humanists first proposed their theories about therapy in the late 1950s and early 1960s. The humanists objected to Freudian and cognitive–behavioral therapies, which were very hierarchical (the therapist was seen as the expert doctor who fixed the patient) and focused only on pathology.

Today, all types of therapy are much more collaborative in nature, seeing both therapist and client as bringing expertise to the process, and focusing, at least in part, on building on each client's natural ability and strengths. However, at the time, the humanists' belief that the client was the expert in his own life and had the power to change himself was radical, as was their shift in therapy from a focus on mental illness to a focus on growth and fulfillment. The concept of "self-actualization"[7] means growing into one's fullest potential as a human being. Rather than merely reducing suffering, as Freud attempted to do, the humanists encouraged this type of growth.

In many ways, the humanistic approach is more a philosophy than a strategy for doing therapy. Important concepts include freedom, responsibility, and the value of authenticity (by which the humanists meant being self-aware and truthful) both in the therapeutic relationship and as a goal for clients. Humanists are often categorized as client-centered, existential, or experiential.

Freedom and Responsibility

Humanists ascribe strongly to the principle of freedom. We are not bound by our past to operate or respond in certain ways. We have the freedom to choose our relationship to ourselves and the world. Accompanying this freedom is the notion of responsibility for our choices.

Client-Centered Therapy

Therapists using the client-centered approach[8] assume that people's difficulties in life come from having experienced *conditional positive regard* from their caretakers—that is, caring that obligated them to be or act in expected ways in order to receive it. They further believe that everyone will naturally move toward their highest potential in the context of a relationship with someone who offers the opposite—*unconditional positive regard.* The therapist's role is to offer the client both warmth and empathy, and it is important that the therapist be authentic with the client when sharing what he or she is thinking or feeling about that client.

Client-centered therapy does not aim to solve a particular set of problems but to help the person grow so that she can live life more fully, able to deal with specific challenges she faces in multiple ways. There is little emphasis on techniques, other than *empathic reflectivity,* whereby the therapist tries to reflect back to the client an understanding of both the content of and subjective experience expressed in what she is saying. The therapist assumes that this technique helps the client arrive at her own conclusions about herself. The conversation looks much like we saw in the conversations between José, Ernesto, and Rose in the discussion of psychodynamic therapy. However, the client-centered therapist would not interpret the client's words or actions for unconscious meaning, as a psychodynamic therapist might do.

EXISTENTIALISM

Like the client-centered approach, existentialism is more of a philosophy than a strategy for doing therapy. Anxiety and guilt are considered universal, necessary, and useful—but sometimes debilitating. Suffering, isolation, and death are all inevitable aspects of being human that can be addressed in either life-enhancing or life-restricting ways. The therapist's job is to be authentic with the client and to help the client live

an authentic life, facing and accepting these realities, which
are core to human existence. Working with all of these realities is part of the ongoing process of finding one's meaning,
or purpose, for living. (In Chapter Ten, I discuss these life
conditions in more depth, and offer stories illustrating how
clients experience and work with them.)

Experientialism

Experientialism covers a wide range of therapies, many of
which are not talk therapy, the subject of this book. The focus of all of them, however, is to help clients understand
themselves on more than an intellectual basis. Experiental-
ism stresses that early limbic memories are stored not only
in the mind but in the body, as physical sensations. A basic
premise is that the past is alive in the present and can be addressed through deep awareness of every aspect of the present
experience.

A good example of an experiential talk therapy is Gestalt.[9]
Therapists using this approach pay attention to the *what* and
how of behavior rather than the *why*. They use various techniques to draw attention to the client's awareness of his
senses and his body. For example, the therapist might ask a
client to exaggerate a clenching jaw or jiggling leg, perhaps
asking that part of the body to speak for itself, explaining
what message it wants to give.

A very popular technique taken from Gestalt is the *empty
chair* technique. The client imagines that someone from his
past, or an aspect of himself, is in the chair next to him, and
he talks to that person or part. Or, he can move from chair to
chair, acting out the person or part represented by each.

Ernesto tried this technique in his work with José. Ernesto imagined his father in one chair while he sat in the other and spoke to him, moving back and forth as he played first himself and then his father.

Ernesto—self: Papa, you scare me so much when you yell like that. I feel like I'm nothing in your eyes.

Ernesto—father: Of course you're something. I want you to believe that! Don't you see I just want you to do the best you can?

Ernesto—self: But I don't! I just start feeling bad!

Ernesto—father: I don't want you to feel bad. I want you to *do well.* You have to do well. Don't you understand?

Ernesto—self: No. I mean yes. I know I should do well. And I want to. But I don't think you believe in me.

Ernesto—father: It's not you, it's them.

Ernesto—self: Who?

Ernesto—father: The white people. Your bosses. Your teachers. They'll think you're just a lazy Mexican. I see it every day at work. Who do you think gets laid off first on the job? It's always the Mexicans. That's why I always work over-time. To prove that I'm not like that. I don't want you to let them keep you down! To let them stop you!

Ernesto—self: I understand, Papa. But when you yell at me and tell me I won't amount to anything, I just feel like I won't—like there's nothing I can do to succeed.

As he sat in his father's chair, Ernesto began to feel more compassion for his father, and to understand better what his father wanted for him. When acting as himself, Ernesto was able to tell his father how frightened and hurt he was by his father's anger. This was empowering for Ernesto, who felt like he could take care of the part of himself that still felt

like a child by speaking for and standing up for that child—
something Ernesto had never been able to do before.

THE FAMILY SYSTEMS APPROACH

Family therapy means that more than one member of the
family is in therapy with you. *Family systems theory* is a way
of thinking about the way families function. In Chapter
Five I discuss three modes of therapy: individual, couple or
family, and group. In this chapter, we consider some of the
principles behind family systems theory.

Family systems theory is based on general systems theory, which proposes that the whole is bigger than its individual parts. That is, the interaction among the parts of
any system, whether mechanical or living, produces its
own entity that is more powerful and looks different from
any of the individual parts taken separately. Because they
are all connected, any change in one part of the system—
in this case, the individual members of the family—will
affect the others.

Originally, family theorists focused only on the family system itself. In more recent years, they have included the
larger systems of community and society, which have an
enormous impact on the family.

There are several schools of family systems therapy.[10] The
key feature of all of them is understanding people in the
context of their families and relationships, rather than seeing them only as individuals with their own ways of viewing
themselves and the world. Some schools focus on family history, even looking back several generations, to help people

see the larger context that helped shape them, their lives, and their current families. Others focus primarily on current interactions. Still others focus primarily on possibilities of what could be different in the future.

In this chapter we consider concepts that all family systems therapists might use.

CHANGE VERSUS STAYING THE SAME

Families move between states of flux and times of stability. Both are essential, and too much of either can cause a problem. Ernesto and Rose talked with José about how this issue has affected them since the beginning of their marriage.

José: One of the things you've mentioned is that you always have more fights around the holidays. What happens then?

Rose: It started when we first got married, and it's never changed. We had a fight that very first Christmas. And every year it comes up again.

José: What was the issue?

Rose: We both had our traditions, you know? When we opened presents, when we had the big meal, going to Mass—all that kind of thing. The big problem was that we did those things at the same time. Both our families had a meal and opened presents on Christmas Eve and then went to Mass.

José: So I guess the problem was where the two of you would be, huh?

Rose: Exactly. Ernesto's family is really large, and most of them live right around here. My parents live here in town and I have just one sister who lives out of town and comes in for the holidays. But his family were all upset when we spent that night with my family, even though we suggested that we'd all get together with Ernesto's family on Christmas day.

José: What were they upset about?

Rose: It was like I was taking Ernesto away from them. They couldn't even agree to a plan where we'd alternate years. It just had to be their way, or Ernesto and I were doing it wrong.

José: Ernesto, would you describe it the same way?

Ernesto: Pretty much. My mother makes a big feast. It's really important to her that we're there. And important to everyone else, too. It hurt my family so much to think we wouldn't be there at that special time.

José: Rose, how did your family react?

Rose: They thought it was okay that we trade. That we'd do Christmas day instead of Christmas Eve on the alternate years. And that seemed reasonable to me. But then because Ernesto's family was so upset, Ernesto just kept saying, "Well, your family doesn't care as much." And then besides, it's easier for my family to change because there's fewer of them. If his family changed, all sorts of people would have to change. So we always end up over there on Christmas Eve. My family tries to do Christmas day, and it works okay, but it's harder. Lots of times my sister has to run back and forth between my parents' house and her in-laws.

José: What do you think of that?

Rose: I can sort of see it, but it just seems unfair! How come they get to always have it their way? It ruins the holiday for me. I just feel bad.

José: Ernesto, it sounds like you're stuck. You either have to hurt your family or hurt Rose.

Ernesto: Yes. I wish my family could be flexible about it, but it would be a lot harder for them, like Rose said. Then they start acting like I don't care about them if I don't come. Or they blame Rose for taking me away. It hurts.

José: I bet it does.

Ernesto: I get upset that she wants to do something that will make them angry at both of us—and especially at her. I want them to get along. I want them to love Rose, not resent her.

José: Is it easier to put pressure on Rose than to tell your family how you and she are going to do things?

Ernesto: I guess so. It matters more to them.

Rose: But it matters to me, too! It's not fair!

Ernesto: I know, but you see what they do when we don't come. I don't want them to be hurt—or to hurt us.

José: I think you're trying to make the best of things, Ernesto. It sounds like you think the consequences of angering or hurting your family are worse than hurting Rose. What do you think?

Ernesto: Yeah, that makes sense. We fight, but then we get over it. If I disappoint my family, they go on and on about it for weeks.

José: Rose, what do you think of that?

Rose: It makes me mad. Why should they get their way just because they're more rigid about it?

José: I think that's a good question. And we should look at whether it makes sense to continue to handle the issue in the same way.

The tension for Ernesto and Rose arose because Ernesto's family could not change their expectations to accommodate the fact that Ernesto had married, and now they had to take into account not only their tradition, but his wife's and her family's. They saw his change as a betrayal rather than a natural evolution.

On the other extreme are families whose expectations change constantly or unpredictably, leaving family members disoriented and anxious. Although Rose's family looked more reasonable than Ernesto's, it turned out that as a child, Rose often didn't know what to expect from her parents, particularly her father, whose moods were unpredictable. One day her father was quiet and easygoing, letting Rose and her sister do whatever they wanted. The next day he might shout at, or even beat, his daughters for the same behavior he had accepted without question the day before. Weeks could go by during which no one ate supper at the same time, with everyone just grabbing something from the fridge whenever it was convenient. Suddenly their mother would seem shocked and hurt that everyone had plans and wouldn't be available to eat Sunday night dinner together.

As Rose, José, and Ernesto continued to discuss the Christmas fight, Rose began to see that part of what upset her so much was that the Christmas Eve tradition was one of the few rituals she could count on as a child. She didn't want to lose it.

Boundaries

Boundaries are the fences that families create, both between family members and between the family and the outside world. How strongly marked those boundaries are varies from family to family. Although certain behavior—for example incest—is considered a boundary violation in every culture, the definition of appropriate or healthy family boundaries, like most other aspects of family dynamics, is strongly influenced by cultural norms.

The boundaries between family members determine how much and what kind of information they share with each other, how much time they spend together, and the degree to which privacy and autonomy are tolerated for each member of the family. Families may have relatively open boundaries in one of these areas but very closed boundaries in another.

The Diaz family had very open boundaries with regard to sharing information and spending time together. Rose learned early on than anything she said to one member of the family would quickly become general knowledge. No one kept a confidence. In addition, the grown children all lived near one another and their parents and the family spent much of each weekend together. Ernesto recalled that if he went to his room to read when he was a child, his family would tease him for not joining them. However, Ernesto's sister Alejandra told Rose that no one talked about their real feelings. There was a lot of teasing and a lot of boisterous arguments about politics and sports, but any show of vulnerability was off-limits.

All of this was a source of surprise and discomfort for Rose. In her family, people valued privacy and private time. Often when everyone was home they were in different rooms. No one would ever dream of passing on information obtained from one family member to another without getting explicit permission. Her family was like her in-laws in one important way, however: few people in Rose's family shared personal pain with one another. A stiff upper lip was the norm. The only strong emotion expressed was her father's sporadic anger.

Boundaries can often differ from person to person within the same family. One person's feeling of closeness might be another's feeling of being smothered. For many people in therapy, it is important to identify their own comfort level with regard to boundaries; learning when and how to ask for what they want, especially when others' needs are different from theirs; and learning when and how to honor the needs of others.

Ernesto was close to his mother, but he often experienced her as intrusive. She wanted him to tell her everything, like his sisters did. She'd get hurt—even cry—when Ernesto would refuse. The tension between them heated up after Ernesto married Rose. He and José discussed the problem:

José: So you feel squeezed, sometimes. Your mother wants in on your personal life and you don't want to let her in.

Ernesto: Right. I love Mama. But she wants to know too much—things that aren't her business. You know, like what's happening with me and Rose.

José: And now it's doubly complicated. Not only are you reluctant to tell her those details, but Rose probably doesn't want you to. Is that right?

Ernesto: Absolutely. No matter what I do, one of them is mad at me. My mother complains I'm keeping her out of my life. Rose complains that I tell my mother way too much.

José: Sounds like the Christmas fight. You're stuck again, trying to please them both.

Ernesto: Uh-huh.

José: What I'm hearing is that this difference between you and your mother was there before Rose came along. Right?

Ernesto: Yes. She always got so hurt when I wouldn't tell her about my friends, my girlfriends, what I'm doing. . . .

José: I think that's important to remember. Part of our work together needs to be helping you figure out what you want. When two people you love want competing things from you, it's easy to start thinking that your only problem is that they disagree. It's easy to forget that you have to get clearer about where you want to set your own limits. Does that make sense?

Ernesto: Well, . . . sort of. I mean, I have to respect Rose's wishes about keeping things private, don't I?

José: Yes, of course. It wouldn't be good for your relationship for you to share things about her that she'd rather you didn't. But if there was something you really wanted to tell your mother, maybe you and Rose could talk about it. Maybe there'd be a way to decide together what you'd say to your mother. The first step would be you deciding

what seems right to you. Then you and Rose would have something
to work with. Right now it seems like you're mostly focusing on what
they want, not what you want.

Ernesto: That's certainly true.

Boundaries also separate the family from the outside
world. Some families' boundaries are very thick, letting no
one into the family's inner sanctum. On the other extreme
are families with extremely permeable boundaries, so that
one might have trouble being able to tell who is a member of
the family and who a guest.

FAMILY ROLES AND RULES

Everyone has various roles in the family. Some roles come
with an official title, such as sister, parent, or uncle. Others,
such as caretaker, confidante, or rebel, evolve from the relationships among family members.

Strongly related to family roles are rules. These rules are
generally, but not always, unspoken. They govern how people play their roles and what roles they adopt. Rules govern
what feelings are acceptable to show, or even to have;
whether people are expected to attend family events; what
girls or boys are supposed to be like; whether sex is an acceptable topic for conversation; how people use money; and
so on. Although every family has rules, every individual
member doesn't necessarily ascribe to them. This is further
complicated when people marry, combining two families'
rules. With blended families, often three or more families'
rules get mixed together.

We've already seen examples of some family rules in our
discussions of Ernesto and Rose. For example, Ernesto's
family has a strong rule about attending a family event such

as Christmas Eve. If you don't, you risk, as Ernesto did, great anger and hurt and the accusation that you are betraying the family. Both Ernesto's and Rose's families have the rule that one doesn't share feelings, except for anger, and that seems to be a feeling that only males express—Ernesto's and Rose's fathers, then Ernesto, and now Alberto.

In Rose's thought chart in the section on CBT, it's clear that she believed that, in order to be a good mother, she had to make Alberto behave. This is also one of her family's rules about how to play the role of mother.

In therapy, a big job is identifying what roles you play and what your family rules are. Then you decide whether and how you want to play your assigned roles and what other family rules make sense to follow. For example, José noted that Rose and Ernesto would do well to consider changing how they currently handle the Diaz family rule about Christmas Eve. Rose challenged the rule. Why is it fair, she asked, to have to do it the Diaz way just because they'll be upset? And, José observed, it's a good question. The job in therapy is to try to discern whether the rule is a good one to honor or whether, in fact, it's harmful. The Diaz family's rule that not showing up for Christmas Eve is a sign of betrayal, even when it means missing Rose's equally important ritual with her own family, may be a harmful rule that Rose and Ernesto would do well to challenge.

TRIANGLES: THREE'S A CROWD

Triangles are interactions between three people or groups of people in a family. We often bring in a third party when we're having trouble with someone in our family. This can be useful if it helps us blow off some steam and decide how we want to resolve the issue. But triangles can become problematic when we get stuck in them.

Recall that Rose and Ernesto first came to therapy because of their concerns about Alberto's behavior. Ernesto often felt that Rose didn't follow through on the limits they agreed upon. This dynamic has the makings of a classic family triangle. As José observed, it looked like Rose might be unconsciously encouraging Alberto to express the anger she was afraid to express with Ernesto. Had they not come to therapy and begun work on their relationship, they could have gotten stuck there, focusing on concerns about Alberto rather than dealing more directly and effectively with their conflicts as a couple.

FAMILY SECRETS

All families have information that they keep private from the outside world, and even from individual members. Parents, for example, typically don't share financial issues with young children. Family secrets, however, are filled with emotional charge. Families who keep secrets usually do so because they feel ashamed about something—for example, drug abuse, affairs, or incest. Discovery of family secrets can be devastating to family members who were unaware of their existence. Furthermore, sharing them with someone outside the family—or, in some cases even talking about them out loud to other family members—can be regarded as a sign of profound disloyalty.

As José, Ernesto, and Rose continued their work, they discussed what might be behind Rose's father's erratic moods. As she described him in more detail, José began to suspect that her father might have a mental illness. Rose remembered a few times in her childhood when he was gone for several weeks. No one had ever talked about where he was. She recalled asking her mother and getting very vague responses, such as, "He's on a trip." José encouraged her to see if she could learn more.

It turned out that Rose's mother was willing to disclose more about those early days. Rose was shocked to learn that her father had actually been hospitalized—twice for serious depression and twice because he was acting erratically and destructively. He'd stayed up for days at a time, driving recklessly and drinking heavily—something he rarely did at other times. Both her parents had been very ashamed of his problems, and neither had told anyone in the family or their community what had happened.

In recent years, doctors finally figured out the most effective medication for Rose's father, so he no longer had trouble with severe mood swings. Also, Rose learned that he had had some therapy sessions and that her mother had even joined him for some. Her parents had thought about talking to Rose and her sister about the history, but didn't know how to bring it up. They were glad that Rose came to them.

Learning about this was a big relief for Rose, who had never been able to make sense of her experiences with her father. It was also a relief—and very healing—to finally talk about the unacknowledged cloud over the family, first with her mother, and, later, with her father. Her father told her how sorry he was that he had hurt Rose and her sister. Those conversations meant a lot to Rose, who was able to forgive her father's abuse and to understand that his anger was not a reflection of who she was or how he felt about her.

THE THERAPEUTIC RELATIONSHIP

The use of the therapeutic relationship in family systems therapy tends to reflect the school or schools of thought to which the family systems therapist subscribes. For many, especially when working with an individual, it is similar to the psychodynamic approach. Although the focus on the relationship between client and therapist is less central in family therapy when there are multiple family members in the room, it is nonetheless considered important. How family members react to the therapist and how the therapist feels in the family's presence are information that can help people understand and resolve old issues that affect the current situation. Other systems therapists play the role of director or coach, focusing less on using their own reactions to the family as a resource and more on techniques to help individuals and family members improve their sense of themselves and their relationships with one another.

TECHNIQUES

Depending on a therapist's school of thought, he may use any number of family systems techniques. For example, he may encourage you to try an experiential exercise to demonstrate your family interactions. At one point, José suggested that Rose and Ernesto do such an exercise. As they described the nature of their fights—the way in which Rose would retreat when Ernesto got angry—José suggested that they act it out by standing in a way that represented their positions during the arguments. Rose stood up, walked to the corner of the room, and turned her back to Ernesto. Ernesto placed himself in the middle of the room, walking toward Rose with his arms reaching out to her, unable to touch her. Then Ernesto abruptly turned and walked angrily in the other direction. The physical experience of their interaction allowed them to talk more freely about what typically happened and how they'd like it to change.

Another therapist might ask you to do some research on the family in which you were raised, to learn about multigenerational patterns. She might suggest that you ask questions of your extended family members—siblings, cousins, aunts, uncles, and grandparents—that will give you a sense of family roles, rules, attitudes, and boundaries. You can also ask questions to learn about patterns such as divorce, alcoholism, or abuse; or about the family's ongoing values, for instance, that religion, art, education, or financial success are highly prized.

As illustrated by José's work with Ernesto and Rose, these four approaches—psychodynamic, cognitive–behavioral, humanistic, and family systems—are quite compatible with one another. Although, for example, the psychodynamic approach explicitly focuses on the unconscious, the use of a CBT strategy to explore a client's core beliefs underlying a "hot" automatic thought will often uncover material that the client did not previously recognize. Exploration using either the psychodynamic or the CBT approach often leads to information about the client's family. As the existentialists suggest, anxiety and guilt are part of the human condition. Any approach can lead a client to awareness of, and ways for facing and dealing with, those issues. All of these approaches help the client develop a new and expanded narrative of who he is and what his life is all about. Many therapists draw from several approaches, as José did, sometimes focusing more on one than the other, depending on their style and the client's needs.

Some, however, clearly prefer one approach over others. My colleague Jacob prefers the CBT approach, which he says is a better fit for his style—he describes himself as a "problem solver." He also thinks that the structure and use of concrete techniques such as the Thought Record help clients see him and the process of therapy as more credible, thus increasing their belief that it will be helpful. In contrast, my colleague Arlene believes that psychodynamic theory explains clients' complex and subjective experience of life more accurately than the others, and she thinks that bringing the unconscious to light is a key aspect of helping people change. In addition, she thinks it is essential to make explicit use of the phenomenon of transference in her work with clients. Most of what she does is grounded in psychodynamic theory. Ultimately, each client must decide which therapist, and which approach or approaches, are the best fit.

CHAPTER 7

Modes of Therapy

Who's in the Room?

Although your psychotherapy is about you, working one-on-one with your therapist is not your only option. Some clients opt for family therapy, others for group therapy. Let's take a close look of each of these three options.

COMING ALONE: INDIVIDUAL THERAPY

Individual therapy has several advantages. Probably the biggest one is that you have complete control over what you talk about and who knows about it. This control gives you the freedom to explore some things that you might be afraid to approach if you had to say them out loud in front of your friend, partner, child, or parent and face his or her reactions to it, which can make it difficult to follow something potentially scary to its conclusion.

Another advantage is that the time is all yours. You don't have to share it with anyone. Rarely are we in a situation where we get another person's undivided attention. Rarely do we even give this to ourselves.

COMING WITH SOMEONE IN YOUR FAMILY: FAMILY THERAPY

People in individual therapy often invite important people in their lives—parents, partners, adult or minor children—to join them in some therapy sessions. This helps everyone to gain a new perspective on their relationships or to change some aspect of these relationships. Others—mostly couples, but sometimes family groups—decide to seek therapy together. (Unfortunately, too many couples wait until they are at the point of deciding whether or not to stay together. It is far better to come in for help while both are committed to making the relationship work.)

In family therapy you lose the control and privacy that you have in individual therapy. For this reason, many are reluctant to do it. It feels too risky. However, there are great advantages that make it well worth the risk. First, if you are talking to your therapist alone about a relationship, even if you try your best to represent the other person fairly and accurately, you can't completely do it. We can only see another person through our own eyes, and, when we are emotionally charged, our vision is affected. Your therapist has the advantage of not being emotionally involved. Thus, she is likely to see things you can't, and she can offer you a new perspective on the situation. Or, if you don't trust your perceptions of others, your therapist might affirm that your perception is reasonable.

Ironically, the very thing that makes it scary to engage in couple or family therapy is also what makes it safe and extremely helpful. Usually, when we talk to family members about upsetting or difficult issues outside a therapist's office, it's hard to truly hear what the other person has to say or to believe that she hears you. And because the conversation feels risky, we often find it hard to say what's on our minds. We may send very unclear messages, say things we don't really mean, beat around the bush, or say hurtful things out of fear or pain, rather than because we really believe what we're saying. Or, perhaps, we say nothing at all. All of these possibilities lead to interactions that are unproductive at best, destructive at worst.

But your therapist will work hard to hear and understand what the world is like from everyone's point of view and to help everyone hear each other. It's often easier to say things that you are scared to say if you know someone is there to help you say it and to help others in the family hear it. Your therapist will help each person see his or her impact on others, and hold each person accountable for treating others fairly.

When Rose and Ernesto first began therapy, José asked each of them to talk to him, rather than each other, about what was bothering them. He asked that when one was talking, the other simply listen, without responding. He began this way because he suspected that Rose and Ernesto, like most couples in conflict, were reacting to each other out of their own pain and fear. Neither could really hear the other. And neither could say what was on their minds, because they anticipated the other's usual response.

The conversation went like this:

José: Rose, can you describe how you feel when Ernesto raises his voice?

Rose: I get really scared.

José: What scares you?

Rose: He gets so mean when he's angry. He starts telling me everything that's wrong with me.

José: It sounds like you're scared that he's going to hurt your feelings. Is that true?

Rose: Uh-huh. I start to feel real bad about myself. Like I'm no good in his eyes.

José: What usually happens to you then?

Rose: I just want to hide. I feel so bad I don't know what to say anymore. And if I keep talking to him, he just keeps getting madder and madder.

José: So you just stop talking?

Rose: Yes. I shut up. And try to go to another room to be alone.

José: Does that help?

Rose: Well, in a way. At least after a while he stops yelling. But I still feel bad about what he said. And usually we end up not talking for a long time. I hate that. I feel so apart from him then.

José: It sounds like hiding feels like your only choice, to escape feeling hurt by him, but you still feel pretty terrible.

Rose: I don't know what else to do. I love Ernesto. I really do. He's so kind and fun most of the time. I just don't know what to do when things get bad like that. And I think Alberto feels the same way. It hurts me so much to see how much he loves his father and wants his approval.

At this point, José turned to Ernesto.

José: Ernesto, what's it like for you to hear that Rose loves you?

Ernesto: It's great. But she sure doesn't act that way sometimes.

José: What do you mean?

Ernesto: She ignores me. She walks away. Refuses to talk.

José: So when Rose goes and hides, as she puts it, it looks to you like she doesn't love you. Is that right?

Ernesto: I'd say so. She just won't listen.

José: I bet that makes you even more upset.

Ernesto: Of course. It makes me angry. A wife should respect her husband. And Alberto does the same thing. He just acts like I'm not there. I think she puts him up to it.

José: It sure doesn't feel like you and Rose are on the same team as parents
        then.

Ernesto: No. She undercuts me.

José: How does she do that?

Ernesto: Like I told you before. We decide that Alberto needs to be pun-
           ished. Then she just goes behind my back and gives him what he
           wants.

José: That must really make you think she doesn't respect you.

Ernesto: Yeah—she acts like I'm just a failure. Like I don't know what I'm
           doing. It hurts. You know?

José: Of course, it does. Sounds like both of you feel that the other is say-
        ing that you're no good or a failure, and that both of you get hurt by
        that. Anyone would. But it looks to me like neither one of you has ac-
        tually said that or actually feels that way. Ernesto, I'm wondering if
        it makes a difference when you hear Rose say that she hides because
        she feels hurt and scared, not because she doesn't respect you.

Ernesto: Well . . . I suppose it does. I'm not trying to hurt or scare her. I'm
           trying to be a good father.

José: A lot of times in marriage we don't know that our wife or husband is
        hurt or scared. Often we're too caught up in our own feelings to notice
        each other's. Rose, did you realize that your hiding hurts Ernesto?

Rose: Not really. He just always seems so mad and like he doesn't care
        what I think. I never thought about him being hurt.

José: It looks like neither of you were aware of how badly you wanted each
        other's respect and support. I want to say again, that's really common.

This realization was important for Ernesto and Rose. Rose
had no idea that she had any impact on her husband. She
was happy to hear that her opinions and support were important to him, and she began to see how withdrawing and
ignoring their agreements about Alberto reinforced his own
self-doubt as a parent and as a man. She genuinely respected

him and was able, for the first time, to let him know this in a way that he could hear.

Ernesto saw, for the first time, how his anger scared Rose and contributed to her self-doubt and her desire to withdraw. Their conversation in therapy gave Ernesto and Rose the skills to talk with each other far more effectively, to support one another, and to treat each other with compassion and respect.

YOU'RE NOT ALONE: GROUP THERAPY

Group therapy, like family therapy, involves more than one person. It carries some of the same disadvantages as family therapy: You are called upon to share your personal experience with others who might have negative reactions, and attention is not focused solely on you. However, unlike family therapy, group members are not related to you and, usually, aren't people you know in any other context. They are like your therapist in that you can safely explore who you are with them and experiment with new ways of acting and responding before trying them out in your regular life.

As individual clients do in their one-to-one sessions with therapists, group members tend to create a microcosm of their lives within the group. However, because there are more participants, there are more people to represent each client's world. This multiplicity opens the door to greater understanding and more opportunities to experiment with new ways of responding. Whereas in real life people often don't tell you their reactions to you or respond in ways that aren't helpful to you, in group therapy, as in family therapy, you have the chance to hear and learn from others, with the help of a therapist who can help you hear more clearly and help others speak more constructively.

In addition to providing feedback from peers, groups offer you the opportunity to learn from others' experience. Quickly you find that even when the focus is on someone else, the discussion and interaction are helpful to you. Also, because people often feel they are alone in their suffering, being in a group allows us to see that others share similar experiences and struggles. Seeing others master their challenges gives you the confidence that you will be able to do so as well.

Some groups include a mix of genders, cultures, ethnicities, and issues. Other groups are more focused, with all members being, for example, male, African-American, or lesbian. Or perhaps everyone in a group is working on experiences related to sexual abuse, or eating disorders, or grief. Some groups are ongoing, with people entering and leaving at different times, but staying for an extended period, perhaps 6 months to a year or more. Others are time limited, with everyone beginning and ending at once. Still others are time limited, but with people beginning and ending at different points, so there are always people at different stages of progress in the group at the same time.

Your regular attendance in group therapy sessions is very important not only for you, but for the other members of the group. They count on you being there for them.

In most situations, contact among group members outside of the group is discouraged—or there are clear expectations for what kind of contact people will have and how people will address it in the group. This is important in order to keep the group safe for all members. If two people form a tight friendship outside of the group, this may negatively affect the way they relate to each other and to other members, especially during therapy sessions. A final aspect of safety is that group members are expected to keep confidential any information about other members of the group.

A GROUP THERAPY EXPERIENCE: RASHAN'S GROUP FOR FATHERS

Rashan led a group for African-American fathers. The group's eight members met on a weekly basis for 4 months. Below are some of the experiences the men had in the course of their work.

Delmar was the oldest son of five children. Their father disappeared when he was 11, and he was often left with the responsibility of caring for his younger siblings. The best job their mother could get was on a night shift, so when the children were home, she was often sleeping. At an early age, Delmar learned how to take charge and help others.

Now a father himself, he joined Rashan's group. He offered very insightful feedback to others and suggested useful strategies they could try in their lives, acting more like a cotherapist than a client. However, he never brought up concerns of his own. When other group members commented on his behavior, he found a way to change the subject, usually by pointing to their own failings in some way. Eventually group members became angry at his superior attitude. They all were trying to be better fathers, and Delmar acted like he had it all together. Their anger was familiar to Delmar, whose younger brothers had been in a lot of trouble, some of them getting involved with gangs and drugs. No matter how hard Delmar tried to set them straight, he failed. Instead of appreciating his guidance as an older brother, they threw it back in his face.

Rashan recognized that Delmar was recreating his family dynamics in the group. Whereas Delmar's brothers dismissed his advice and treated him with outright contempt at times, Rashan helped the group members make specific—and nonblaming—statements about what they saw Delmar doing and its effect on them. Perry, a member who had initially liked his insight, said he was beginning to think that Delmar would not value anything he had to say. As a result, Perry told Delmar, he became less willing to seek Delmar's feedback and, in fact, found himself automatically rejecting it.

Delmar tried to deflect the feedback by turning the issue back to the group, as he had before, but Rashan kept asking him to speak about how he felt upon receiving it. Eventually Delmar was able to acknowledge that the feedback stirred up old feelings of being overwhelmed by the need to be in charge and his sense that there was no room for him to have needs of his own. Early on, as a way to protect himself, he learned to hide, even from himself, the fact that he might have needs at all.

He also talked about his pain at having his best efforts so constantly rejected by his brothers. Rashan and the group all let him know that, as an 11-year-old, he could not possibly do it right—the job assigned to him was far beyond the capabilities of any child that age. They also helped him understand, by explaining their own reactions, why his brothers might have wrongly blamed Delmar for not being the father they all desperately needed and sorely missed. Finally they helped him see the social pressure on him as a man, and in particular as an African-American man, to show no weakness and assume no one would support him.

Malik had grown up in a family where children's needs were not recognized. Although both of his parents were in the *home, they struggled with poverty and often felt beaten down by the racial discrimination they came to expect. Malik was always a good student in school, but he felt that he got little support from his parents, who rarely showed up for school events, even ones in which he played an important role.*

Like Delmar, Malik found ways to protect himself, in his case by working two jobs to provide for his family financially. Although his wife appreciated what he did, she was hurt that he rejected her offers of emotional support as well as her offer to work more hours so that he could be at home more. He was driven by a need to prove himself. If his wife worked more or if he leaned on her for emotional support, he would be a failure as a man. He watched Delmar let in the feedback from the group, begin to recognize the pain behind his behavior, and finally accept support, first from the group and later from others in his life. Delmar's progress gave Malik the confidence that he could do the same.

USING A COMBINATION OF THERAPY MODES

Often people are in more than one mode of therapy at a time. Because of the different emphases of each mode, participating in more than one mode can deepen and strengthen the experience. Here are some questions that may be useful in helping you decide which mode(s) of therapy might be helpful for you.

- Do you want time to sort out things without anyone else (other than your therapist) listening or reacting while you do it?

- Do you feel like you have so much to talk about that it would be difficult for you to share the time you have with others?
- Are you pretty sure that your concerns have more to do with you than with how others in your life are treating you?
- Are you in a troubling relationship with someone who is unwilling to work with you about it?

If you answered "yes" to some of these questions, individual therapy is likely an excellent option.

- Do you want to work on your relationship with a particular person or group of people in your family or with a friend or intimate partner?
- If so, are those people willing to join you in therapy?

If you answered "yes" to both of these questions, then couple or family therapy would likely be beneficial.

- Do you want to know more about what it's like for others who share some of the same challenges in life that you face?
- Do you want to find out more about your impact on other people?
- Do you want a place where you can experiment with other ways of responding to people?

If you answered "yes" to some of these questions, group therapy may be very helpful for you.

Some therapists are willing to work in a variety of modes. For example, they might work with a couple or with various members of a family in different combinations, sometimes seeing one or more members individually, and sometimes seeing some or all of them together. Some therapists facilitate the groups to which they refer their clients. Others think it's important that the therapist who sees someone individually be different from the one who sees that same person in couple, family, or group therapy. Therapists base these decisions on their own philosophy about what works best and on what they think will work best for you.

Let's remember, again, that no matter the approach or mode, the goal of therapy is the same: to enhance your well-being and growth by enabling you to gain greater awareness and increased options for relating to yourself and the world. As such, therapy is a process of change. Although not linear, it is possible to understand this process as occurring along a continuum. In the next chapter, I describe this continuum in more depth.

CHAPTER 8

Stages of Change

At any given point in our lives, whether in therapy or not, we are at one or more stages of change.[1] In this chapter, I'll describe each stage to help you identify where you are and how you can use therapy to facilitate these naturally occurring processes.

STAGE #1—PRECONTEMPLATION: NOT THINKING ABOUT IT

The first stage of change is *precontemplation*. To the extent that you are in this stage, you don't think any change is necessary. If you are already seeing a therapist, it was probably someone else's idea.

Sometimes people are ordered to therapy by a court; for example, the authorities may have taken away their children or will do so unless the parents learn to do a more effective job. Sometimes in situations where there has been physical or sexual abuse, the abusers must do therapy as a condition of seeing their children or partners or instead of going to jail. People in this position are called *involuntary* clients.

Although they always have the option of refusing, it means accepting a consequence they may think is worse. These people are almost always in the precontemplation stage. On the other hand, even someone who is very committed to her work in therapy may be, on some level, in precontemplation. All of us are wedded to aspects of ourselves that we are afraid to challenge or change. And all of us have parts of ourselves of which we are unaware—and that we are reluctant to discover.

INVOLUNTARILY VOLUNTARY

I see many clients who come to therapy voluntarily—that is, without being court-ordered—but who really don't want to be in my office, and who don't see any real reason to be there. Usually someone else sees a problem that the client doesn't agree is there. Consider the following two examples.

Sandy was very concerned about Julian's drinking and marijuana use. Although Julian sometimes hid his pot smoking from Sandy, he did so, in his mind, because she overreacted to what he considered moderate use. Sandy came from a family that viewed any substance use as dangerous. She rarely drank alcohol and had never tried pot. She worried about any use, as well as about Julian's evasiveness and, at times, his downright deceitfulness. These qualities reinforced her sense that he was in trouble—and untrustworthy. She wasn't sure that she could stay in the marriage unless Julian got some help. Although Julian didn't agree he had a problem, he did agree to come to therapy.

Don, an emotional and very self-reflective man, found his wife Marcie cool and unresponsive, both sexually and emotionally. It was difficult for her to identify, much less express, what she felt and thought about personal topics. However, she enjoyed Don and thought he treated her well. And she thought they did a good job of raising their three children. She was baffled by Don's sense of loneliness in the marriage, as she was quite happy with the ways things were going, except when he was upset with her. She was shocked when Don said he was seriously considering leaving the marriage unless she agreed to go to therapy.

Although Julian and Marcie each agreed to go to therapy, and therefore are technically voluntary clients, they did not see themselves as needing to change. They went because their spouses had threatened to leave unless they did something. As with those who are court-ordered, the potential consequence seemed worse than therapy.

What to Do

If you find yourself in this situation, it is, first, a good idea to acknowledge that this is how you feel. It's true that therapy does work best when people have an idea of what they'd like to accomplish. That is a challenge when you don't really think you need to be there. However, there are some ways around it. It's worth remembering that you have, in fact, decided to do this rather than face other consequences that seem worse.

My colleague Jan says that when she first meets a client who is in this position, she asks him why the person who insisted he try therapy might be so upset. The client may respond that the other person is really the one with the problem. "She's reacting too much to my drinking." "He's too needy."

"She just can't commit to a relationship." Even when two people are in therapy together voluntarily, each often thinks the other needs to change the most, and hopes that the therapist will see things the same way. Actually, most people's complaints about their partners are fairly accurate. After all, most people know their partners pretty well. Perhaps your partner does have a problem that would be usefully addressed in therapy.

However, this doesn't get you off the hook. Your partner knows *you* pretty well, too. If someone you love has dragged you to therapy because of her concerns about you and your relationship, there's probably some truth to those concerns. You obviously cared enough about the relationship to choose therapy rather than the consequence of not going. Now that you're here, you might as well try to learn more about your partner's concerns and what you may want to do differently. Maybe there are some relatively easy behavioral changes you could make that would make a big difference in how others respond to you. Perhaps you can learn to state your own concerns more effectively, leading to some changes you would like to see in your partner's behavior.

There is a bottom line, however. If you firmly decide that there's nothing in therapy for you, and you see no reason to explore what might be possible through it, then, in fact, you're right. To make use of therapy, you need to be open to its possibilities. And you need to take the process seriously and tell the truth about yourself as best you can. (This truth telling can and should include your skepticism, distrust, and anger about coming to therapy.) If you are unwilling to do this, you don't belong in therapy.

STAGE #2—CONTEMPLATION: THINKING ABOUT IT

After precontemplation is the stage of *contemplation*. Here you are thinking about whether there is something you want to explore or change in yourself. Quite possibly, you're not sure what it is, and you may be very ambivalent about finding out. All of this is fine—and normal. Most people are in the contemplation stage when they begin therapy, and they spend a great deal of their time in this stage during therapy.

RAISING AWARENESS

In therapy, the contemplation stage is a time of consciousness-raising. It's a time for learning more about yourself, your situation, your strengths, your challenges, and your weaknesses. Your therapy might include education about depression, substance abuse and dependency, anxiety, relationships, eating disorders, or the impact of living in various types of family systems with various types of parents. Consciousness-raising also occurs as a result of feedback and guidance from your therapist that allows you to explore your inner world more deeply. During this time, you will become more aware of how you think, feel, and behave; how these three processes affect you and others; and whether you are satisfied with that impact or want it to change.

True contemplation can be very scary because it involves evaluation—sometimes evaluation of your core values, the ways in which you have dealt with life's challenges, your sense of who you are and who you want to be, and your effect on those around you. Being willing to cast a critical eye on the very things that have defined you takes a great deal of courage.

IS IT WORTH THE RISK?

Making the decision to change includes doing a cost–benefit analysis. As you gain clarity about what kinds of changes are possible, you will also face the fact that there are consequences for any change you make.

Elizabeth increasingly experienced her traditional church teachings as hierarchical and patriarchal and felt they no longer provided her with spiritual solace. However, her now-grown sons and her husband of 25 years were all very committed to the tradition. Her husband Jim was a respected leader in the church, and everyone in the congregation thought he was a great guy. Once in therapy, Elizabeth began to discuss her discomfort with the church and her desire to seek other avenues for her own spiritual life. She spoke with her therapist about what might happen if she explored a new and more satisfying spiritual path. She was afraid she would face not only Jim's lack of enthusiasm for her new direction, which she could tolerate, but also his anger at her for rejecting their shared values and, perhaps, his attempts to discourage her. She was also afraid that members of both the church and her family would view her new ideas as heretical, and that she would lose many longtime friendships. Most of all, she worried that her children, who had been her life focus, would reject her if she made this change.

Paul knew something had to change, but he thought that this something was only about him. His wife Sema was a very intelligent, lively, adventurous, and loving woman— everything Paul had ever wanted in a partner. But at several parties, she'd gotten very drunk, and Paul had found her kissing and fondling another man, something she barely remembered doing. She always felt terrible about it the next day, told Paul how much she loved him, and blamed her behavior on the fact that she was drunk. Although Paul rarely drank, most of his friends did, and he wasn't alarmed when someone overdid things occasionally. But it ate at him that Sema had betrayed him, even though he believed her assurances that she didn't do so intentionally. Paul began therapy with the hope that he could learn how to get over his feelings of insecurity about the marriage. He wasn't ready to consider the possibility that the marriage itself was in trouble.

As both of these stories illustrate, if you change yourself or change what you want, you take the risk that others will not accept your change. In fact, I often warn people, "Even if your friends or family tell you they want you to make a change, once you actually make it, they may pressure you to change back." Both psychodynamic and family systems theorists explain this seeming paradox in terms of the agreements we make in our relationships about how each person will behave and what role each will play. We are rarely consciously aware of these agreements. In fact, we often think we want ourselves or others to change, even though, unconsciously, we want things to stay the same.

Some relationships can't survive a change in agreements. It is common, for example, for divorce to occur after an alcoholic becomes sober. Therapists who specialize in chemical dependency have long known that it is a family affair. As much as the alcoholic's partner may hate his drinking and think that all would be solved if only he would stop, the common reality is that sobriety changes the whole relationship, often in ways that are more uncomfortable for the alcoholic's partner. Unless both people are willing and able to work together to forge new agreements, the relationship will falter. Success in changing agreements strengthens the relationship.

People are also ambivalent about change involving how they view themselves. Recall Jake from Chapter Three, who used denial and rationalization to avoid facing his obesity, high blood pressure, and rapid pulse. He eventually realized that his friends' concerns had some validity, and he decided he really wanted to lose weight. But his efforts failed repeatedly; something always seemed to prevent him from doing so. He wasn't sure what it was.

His therapist asked him to consider the possibility that part of him was reluctant to lose weight. What more painful consequence, she asked him, might occur if he were to succeed? Jake and his therapist identified a number of possibilities. Perhaps he wouldn't know what to do when he couldn't use food to comfort himself when he started to feel blue. Possibly, he had used being overweight as a form of protection against the more frightening prospect of sexual and emotional intimacy. As he explored further, Jake realized that over the years, he had repeatedly told himself that if he lost weight he'd be more successful, have more friends, and feel better about himself. Now he had to face the possibility that if he lost weight, maybe none of those things would actually occur. To Jake, such an eventuality would confirm his worst fear: that he was fundamentally unlovable.

If you listen long and carefully enough to anyone's life story, you will discover that the coping skills that person developed are quite logical, even if they look completely self-destructive at first glance. We have all developed coping strategies based on the challenges we face and our internal and external resources. We come to rely on those strategies, especially the ones that have served us well, and they eventually become core parts of ourselves. However, the cliché "Your greatest strength is also your greatest weakness" is a cliché for a reason: It's true. The very things that have served us well are often also the things that cause us our greatest difficulties.

Laticia grew up in a family with very smart parents who were often angry and highly critical and who were unable to acknowledge their contribution to any parent–child conflict. In an effort to avoid their anger and criticism, which she feared and that caused her to feel very ashamed, Laticia became very good at identifying her own failings and, in her words, "confessing to my parents." She believed that if she confessed, they would forgive whatever she had done and not become angry. This effort developed into a skill in which she took great pride—being able to name her part in any conflict and to be completely open and honest about it. Few would argue that this is a bad thing, and she came to see this ability as core to her integrity.

However, during the course of her work in therapy, Laticia became increasingly aware of times when this strategy got her in big trouble. For example, a person who was not equally honest or as willing to be vulnerable would put her at risk of being hurt or taken advantage of. In addition, she began to recognize that, although her hope was that others would not be angry with her, frequently the opposite would occur. Consciously or not, some people felt burdened by the fact that she wanted them to relieve her of her shame. Rather than reassuring her, they become angry in reaction to feeling manipulated.

When challenged in therapy to consider refraining from confessing, Laticia felt a great deal of fear. She anticipated others' anger and disapproval, and she felt that she would betray the foundation of her personal integrity. Challenging this core strategy and the self-identification that went with it was not something she could easily do.

Another reason for ambivalence about changing is plain fear of the unknown. Even if what we do is uncomfortable or gets us in trouble, it's familiar. We know how to do what we do, and we know, more or less, what the results will be.

Change Doesn't Mean You Have to Change Everything

Now for some reassurance. Even if you think you need to consider changing aspects of yourself that you hold dear, it's impossible to completely change your way of doing things—and it's not necessary or wise. Therapy doesn't require you to reject all that you believe in about yourself and the world. Rather, you will be encouraged to examine it all, learn how it works for you and how it doesn't, and consider other alternatives. The goal of this examination is to widen both your awareness and your choices about how to deal with what is in front of you.

Another point of reassurance: How extensively you examine yourself is within your control. You may have no need for such wide-ranging exploration. People frequently go to therapy and successfully resolve a concern within one or two sessions.

Mike, for example, came in because he was having some difficulty figuring out how to respond to his 16-year-old stepson.

A likeable and competent young man, Alan had befriended kids about whom both Mike and his wife had great concerns. Most had no interest in school and at least two had gotten in trouble with the law. Although Mike had been in Alan's life for many years and they'd always had a good relationship, Alan now seemed uninterested in their relationship. In fact, recently he'd become resentful toward Mike. Mike was at a loss about how to approach his stepson.

When his therapist heard Mike's descriptions of his interactions with Alan, it was obvious to her that Mike was missing something: Alan himself had worries about his new friends and revealed these worries to Mike. He probably valued Mike's opinions more than he could allow himself to let on. She also suggested that two important events might be affecting Alan's reaction to Mike. First was the fact that, at 16, Alan was quite naturally becoming more resistant to parental guidance. The second was that Alan's biological father, who had been largely uninvolved with his life for many years, had recently shown much more interest in connecting with his son. Alan might be ambivalent about his father's new interest in him, unsure how to interpret it and whether to trust it. He might even be worried that any overt connection with Mike would threaten the possibility of a deeper relationship with his own father.

Two sessions were enough for Mike to feel more confident about his relationship with Alan and to develop some strategies for supporting Alan's desire for a relationship with his biological father. Mike also found a way to talk with Alan about his new friends and the potential trouble they might bring into his life. Mike is an example of a person moving quickly from contemplation to action, the fourth stage of change.

STAGE #3—PREPARATION: GETTING READY

The next stage is *preparation*, which typically begins about a month before taking action. Preparation is, by definition, getting ready. You begin to make plans to do something different. You may rehearse what you will do with your therapist or with others. You might say out loud what your intentions are, both to your therapist and to others in your life.

Once you announce that you plan to do something, the prospect of doing it becomes more real. At that point someone other than you is expecting something. Even if that person doesn't have a stake in your change, it makes a difference to know that someone is aware of your plan. It's a form of accountability. If you don't do whatever it is you plan to do, someone else will know that you didn't do it.

Elizabeth, who wanted to change her spiritual path, discussed with her therapist the conversations she planned to have with her friends and family, anticipating who would be most likely to support her. She decided that she would start with these people, and then move to those whose reactions she feared the most. She rehearsed with her therapist many conversations with her family, developing some ideas about how she might respond to their questions and concerns.

Laticia told two friends about her tendency to confess and made arrangements to call them for support when she felt the urge to do so. Jake told his brother, who had always been concerned about his weight, that he was starting a serious diet.

All three then took action.

STAGE #4—ACTION: TAKING STEPS

Action is when you actually do something different. Perhaps you've decided to start exercising or stop using drugs. Perhaps you want to change your automatic responses to things that bother you. Perhaps you want to set a limit with someone or keep yourself from setting a limit that you think is unnecessary. Perhaps you want to look for a new job or leave an important relationship. Perhaps you want to have a discussion with someone that you've been scared to have. Perhaps you want to keep yourself from saying what's on your mind. Perhaps you want to start meditating, doing yoga, or going to church.

One of the things that makes people skeptical of therapy is the idea that it's simply "navel gazing." It's true that some people gather a lot of personal insight but never make any tangible changes in how they lead their lives. However, acting just for the sake of acting rarely works—especially if you act before you are really ready, before you've taken the time to contemplate it and prepare for it.

Like all of therapy, action takes courage—that is, doing something you know is good even though you're scared. But, by the time you decide to take action, you've decided that the benefit of doing so outweighs the cost of maintaining the status quo. It's generally true that the more action you take, the more likely you are to succeed in making changes.

People often mistakenly think that they need to wait to act until their fear diminishes. I advise clients that if they do that, they may never act. In fact, the fear is more likely to diminish only once you act. Sometimes the consequences you were worried about don't come to pass. Sometimes you handle them much better than you thought you'd be able to. Sometimes something you don't expect, something quite positive, occurs as a result of your action. At the very least, you have kept a promise to yourself—you've acted in an effort to make your life work better.

Elizabeth's conversations with some of her church friends proved to be very positive. Some of them, it turned out, shared her concerns. They began talking about forming a woman's group within the church community, to share and support each other's spiritual growth. Her conversations with her husband Jim, however, did not go well. He reacted with strong, even harsh, disapproval of her new ideas, and he refused to consider how such a change might contribute something positive to the family. He escalated his attempts to get her to return to being the "woman I married," becoming quite hurt and angry whenever she bought up the topic, and becoming increasingly upset when she connected with her woman friends at church, whom he thought were a bad influence on her.

Although Elizabeth remained committed to her marriage, she began to challenge some of the unspoken agreements that she and Jim had made over the years, and she wondered if they would survive the uproar her challenges were causing. She hoped, in time, that she and Jim could create enough space to support each other in their religious and spiritual journeys. However, she could not return to being who she was before she started to change. She was scared about what this might mean for both of them, but she began to trust that they would both be able to manage it if they had to end their marriage.

Her children were also initially upset with her change. It was particularly painful for her youngest son, who was very close to both of his parents. He was very devout and took his father's side in the conflict. He thought his mother was being selfish and was furious with her. This reaction pushed Elizabeth into a new challenge: learning to stay grounded in what she believed was right in the face of tension between herself and one of her children. Although she knew intellectually that this was healthier than backing off just to avoid the tension, it was very difficult for her. She had to accept that as a parent, she needed to allow her son to have his own experience in life and to come to his own conclusions and positions, even it if meant distance between them.

However, her oldest son expressed interest in what she was thinking and doing. They engaged in some challenging and sometimes painful discussions, and Elizabeth's relationship with him deepened as they talked honestly, perhaps for the first time, about their spiritual and religious beliefs, including doubts and questions about things that were previously considered off-limits to explore.

Laticia began using Thought Records, like the one described in Chapter Six, to help herself move forward. On one occasion, after she'd had a fight with her brother, she noticed that she felt her usual fear and shame. She identified such automatic thoughts as "How can I have such a big mouth?" "What's wrong with me?" and "He's going to be so hurt and angry!" Immediately she wanted to fix the problem in her usual way. She noticed that she had the urge to call him, apologize for hurting him, and tell him the ways she now saw that she had been wrong in the argument. Instead, she challenged her automatic thoughts with alternative thoughts: "I was being honest with my brother, and I did so in a respectful way." "There's nothing wrong with me. I am trying my best to be a good sister." "Even if he's hurt and angry, he'll be okay. And I'll be okay, too. And it doesn't mean I did a terrible thing." This exercise helped diminish the intensity of her shame as well as the degree to which she believed her initial thoughts. However, she was still afraid and still had the urge to fix the problem by confessing.

She called her two friends for support to help her tolerate the discomfort that came with not confessing. She was pleased to discover that she could, in fact, tolerate it, even when her brother was upset with her. She was also happy to notice that when she didn't try to fix the tension between her and others, it tended to dissipate on its own.

Jake found dieting very uncomfortable. As he and his therapist had anticipated, many strong feelings that he had buried through eating began to emerge. However, this led him to a deeper exploration in therapy about what these feelings were and how he might learn to handle them more effectively. For example, he began to examine the roots of his fear of intimacy and to risk becoming more open about himself with his friends. He started to see that, although doing so was difficult, it had its own rewards. He learned that he could count on some of his friends to support him far more than he had ever believed.

Stage # 5—Maintenance: Keeping It Going

Even when we feel like we've really gotten a handle on the changes we've made, it's difficult to stick with them. That's why the final stage—*maintenance*—is so important. Whether the change is something concrete such as no longer drinking, or something less obvious, such as being less reactive to certain emotional triggers, it's often a bumpy road.

During the course of your therapy, and probably during the course of your whole life, you will come back, over and over, to the core issues that brought you to therapy in the first place. We are never perfectly cured—forever freed from anxiety, shame, low self-esteem, or trouble in relationships. All of these things belong to the human condition. But we heal. We learn better ways to cope with them when they emerge. We learn from whom we can get support, what helps us to tolerate and rise above our pain, and how we can avoid things that make us act in harmful ways. We cease our obsessive–compulsive behaviors. We get sober. We stop competing with our brother and replace our struggle with a warm and supportive friendship. We relax and enjoy our lives more.

Where Are You Now?

Here are some questions that can help you determine where you are in the change process, and whether you feel ready to take the next step.

- Are you confused as to why anyone would be worried about, or upset with, you?

- Are you willing to find out if there's anything to be gained from therapy?

If you answered "yes" to the first question, you're in the pre-contemplation stage. If you answered "no" to the second, you won't benefit from therapy unless you change your mind.

- Are you prepared to consider possible consequences that you might face if you make a change?
- Are you prepared to consider the possible consequences of not making a change?
- Do you feel that there is more you need to know before you can decide what changes you want to make?
- Are you interested in finding out what that might be, even if the prospect of learning something uncomfortable scares you?

A "yes" answer to any of these questions suggests that you're in the contemplation stage and ready to engage in the process of building awareness.

- Are you ready to tell someone else what changes you're going to make?
- Are you actively planning ways to make a change?

A "yes" to either of these questions suggests that you're in preparation. Soon you'll be actively making changes.

- Are you taking steps to change your behavior?
- Are you deliberately not reacting to situations from your immediate emotional responses?
- Are you taking steps to change a situation you're in that you don't want to be in? For example, are you applying for a new job?

"Yes" answers to these questions suggest that you are in the action stage.

- Do you feel satisfied with the changes you've made?
- Are you concerned about whether they'll stick?

If these statements are true, it sounds like you're ready to look at how to maintain those changes. It would be good to discuss with your therapist some ways to support the changes you've made.

The change process does not usually happen in a straightforward progression. During the course of your work, you will move back and forth among the five stages, perhaps focusing on the same topic for a while, or perhaps on several. Perhaps you will start to explore something and then back away, like someone in precontemplation, deciding that there's really nothing to examine. Or perhaps you'll make a change and discover something new to look at on the other side of the door.

As you progress, you will probably notice that some overarching themes emerge. The conversations you have with your therapist often involve linking a specific concern you have to one or more of these themes, which may manifest themselves in many areas of your life. As you go back to contemplation, you'll learn more about the ins and outs of the theme, and perhaps consider other actions.

It may be discouraging to hear that we are not perfectly cured of whatever our core stumbling blocks may be. It might help to remember the image of the spiral I described in Chapter One. As we come around and around to ourselves at different junctures in life, we may find ourselves thinking, "This again??? Wasn't this the first thing I talked about in therapy? Didn't I resolve this one? How come it's back?" Notice that, while it may be back, it's back in a different way. We face the challenge with greater awareness and more expanded abilities.

You'll experience the cycle from precontemplation to contemplation, contemplation to preparation, preparation to action and back again not only during therapy, but throughout your life. Once you start down a path that includes a commitment to intentional and honest self-discovery and growth, the path doesn't end. As we mature and life continuously hands us challenges, we are presented with new opportunities to learn how to live our lives in a deeper, more conscious way.

CHAPTER 9

What Can You Do to Enhance Your Therapy?

When therapists are asked what makes for successful therapy, many answer, "Clients who do their homework." By this they mean the things clients do between therapy sessions. The more you carry your therapy out of the therapist's office and into your everyday life (and vice versa), the more you get out of the process. You don't have to do this in an obvious way. In fact, often the process of change requires lots internal percolation that you may never fully realize is happening.

For many of us, the word *homework* connotes something hanging over our heads and, more significantly, something on which we'll be evaluated. Unlike at school or in a job, however, we won't get a grade, promotion, or raise based on how well we perform in therapy. This doesn't mean that there is no process of evaluation in therapy. But your own evaluation of your progress is what counts. *You* are the one who knows whether you are less depressed or less anxious, whether you are making more choices that work for you, whether you are more at peace with things.

In therapy, homework may not involve completing specific tasks. It might simply involve becoming more aware of something and making better (or more conscious) choices. For example, Della, a mother who had been court-ordered to attend therapy, noticed how good it felt when her therapist Helen pointed out things Della did well. She told Helen this, but Helen decided it would be best *not* to use Della's self-observation as an opportunity to talk about how such an experience might be useful to Della with her children, whom she was at risk of losing to foster care. Rather, Helen concluded that Della needed more time to simply absorb the positive experience.

In time, Della started to notice on her own that she was treating her children more positively, imitating the way in which Helen treated her, even though she hadn't actually thought about the connection or consciously decided to behave differently with her children. When Helen invited Della to consider what had helped her change, Della began to see that in caring for her children in the past, she had been repeating a pattern of harsh treatment that she had received from her father. The corrective experience with Helen, she realized, enabled her to change that pattern.

TRACKING

Depending on your therapist's approach and your own best learning style, the types of homework you'll do will range from very concrete to very vague. Some of the best examples of concrete assignments come from those therapists who use a structured cognitive–behavioral approach. Many of these involve tracking actions, emotions, and thoughts, and working with or challenging them. The Thought Record described in Chapter Six is an example. Another involves noting on a chart what you did at various points of each day, what your mood was, and the thoughts you noticed while you did it. After doing this exercise for a while, you'll begin to notice if there are any connections between how you feel, what you're doing, and what you're thinking. Another common type of CBT homework involves working on a specific goal by recording an action plan: when you will begin, what problems you might face, strategies to overcome those problems, and the progress you make. In an effort to reinforce new and more constructive core beliefs, you might do a "historical test"[2] in which you write down experiences you had throughout your life that support a new core belief— evidence that you may have previously ignored. Dennis Greenberger and Christine Padesky's book, *Mind Over Mood: Change How You Feel by Changing the Way You Think* offers an array of exercises such as these, all based on cognitive–behavioral therapy.

WRITING

Often I suggest to clients that they write (but not send, at least not yet) letters to people with whom they have relationships that they would like to change in some way. This can be as simple as wanting to be closer to (or more distant from) the other person. It can also be one-sided, as when the client fully and finally accepts that the other person will never change.

The client then brings the letter into our session and talks about it. Sometimes the client decides to send it, sometimes not, depending on whether he thinks doing so would further the therapeutic process and whether it might damage the relationship with the other person.

Whenever a client decides to send a letter, I help her evaluate whether the letter is written in a thoughtful and respectful manner. It is unethical to encourage a client to send a letter that simply trashes another person, even if that person has been abusive. Such an action does nothing to further the client's relationship with either herself or the other person. On the other hand, if the message is sent in a way that honors the other person's humanity and is not done with a vindictive spirit, it might be a good idea to send it, even if the message it coveys is painful.

My client Eddy wrote such a letter as part of his work in therapy. A man of Swedish descent, brought up in the Lutheran faith, Eddy married Shawna, a Catholic African-American woman. The marriage greatly disturbed Eddy's parents. Eddy had been very close to them and he assumed that, once they got to know Shawna, they'd eventually come around. However, they remained very worried that Eddy's marriage would cause him great difficulty in life. In addition, they felt as if he had betrayed their faith by marrying a Catholic. Shawna understood their discomfort, as her own parents had expressed similar concerns, especially at first. But she was hurt and then angered by what she perceived as Eddy's parents' continued cold treatment of her, even though she had tried to reach out to them. It made her want to stay away. She wanted to support Eddy in his desire to continue the warm relationship he had always had with them, but couldn't help feeling that if he did so, it also meant he accepted their rejection of her. As a result, Eddy and Shawna fought whenever the subject of spending time with Eddy's parents came up.

Eddy had always thought his parents were accepting and kind people, but their reaction to Shawna made him wonder whether they were more prejudiced than he wanted to believe. Whereas in the past he had had an easy and relaxed connection with them, his conversations with them had become increasingly tense. He didn't know how to bridge the gap, especially since he felt he had to choose between his wife and his parents, all of whom he loved.

Recently, Shawna had given birth to their first child. He had always wanted his parents involved in his children's lives, but now the prospect worried him a great deal. Would they be loving grandparents? How could he nurture a relationship with his parents at all, given their attitude toward the mother of his children? He couldn't figure out how, or even whether, to talk with them about it. After some discussion with me, Eddy decided to write his parents a letter.

Dear Mom and Dad,

First let me say that I love you both a great deal. You were great, loving parents to me while I was growing up. I can't imagine what it would have been like if we hadn't been able to have such a close family, including all those wonderful Sunday dinners and holidays at Grandma's. I fully expected that we would have a close relationship once I married and had a family of my own.

The fact that this has not occurred has made me as unhappy as I know it's made you.

As you must know, I love Shawna and our daughter very much, as much as you love each other and me. I do understand your concern about the troubles that both Shawna and I might face because of our mixed marriage. We share those concerns ourselves, and have talked frequently about how to deal with them. I hoped that as you got to know Shawna, you would see what a wonderful woman she is and understand why I decided to share my life with her. Now that we have a child, it hurts me even more to imagine that you might not accept her into your hearts because she isn't baptized as a Lutheran. I'm beginning to think you also object to the color of her skin.

I don't want to choose between my wife and daughter and my parents. I love you so much. But I can't, with any integrity, subject them to a relationship in which they feel like second-class citizens. It's hard for me to believe that my own mother and father may be racist.

I know this letter must be painful for you to read. It is certainly very difficult for me to write. I truly hope we can work this out. If you are willing, I would like to be able talk about it more, perhaps, with the help of a therapist.

With love, Eddy

Eddy brought this letter to therapy and read it to me. He expressed some relief at being able to finally put into words the pain and internal conflict he was feeling. Together, we evaluated whether the letter was both honest and respectful. I suggested that labeling his parents as "racist" would likely hurt them unnecessarily and inflame the situation. I also pointed out that his parents' bias seemed to be about religion, not about race. We talked about how his parents might react

to the letter and whether he wanted to take the risk of sending it. In the end, after deleting the two sentences about
their being racist, Eddy decided to mail it.

Writing a letter that you do send allows you to think carefully, as Eddy did, about what you want to say and how. Often
when we are talking with someone, especially someone with
whom we feel a lot of tension and conflict, we find it difficult
to say what we want to say. We are usually scared, which can
hinder our ability to speak clearly. In addition, because the
other person is reacting to our message, we are simultane-
ously trying to say something difficult and reacting to that
person's reaction to us. The conversation can rapidly spin out
of control. Writing a letter cuts through these difficulties.

Writing a letter can also help the recipient consider the
message carefully, process it, and come up with a response,
without the pressure of having to deal directly with the writer
until she's ready. It's easier to both send and receive a message
if you feel like you aren't called upon to react right away.

As with other risks we take in life, sending such a letter
doesn't necessarily mean that you will get what you hope for.
You can't control another person's reaction. Eddy was fortunate. His parents were able to see how their initial reactions
to his marriage had hurt him and Shawna. Because Eddy
had become increasingly defensive in their conversations
and then had virtually stopped talking with them about
anything of substance, they had assumed that he was angry
at them and didn't care about them and their feelings. They
pulled away, hoping that by doing so, Eddy would eventually
feel comfortable talking to them again. They didn't realize
that both Eddy and Shawna interpreted their behavior as rejection. They thought Shawna was keeping their son away

from them, which added to their initial worries. Eddy's letter opened the door for them to be able to get past the stalemate and start to work through their differences.

Many clients like to keep a journal in which they might include their reactions to a session, their thoughts about it throughout the week, or things that come up during the week that they want to talk about in sessions. Peter, an author, wrote extensively in his journal and often began therapy sessions by reading aloud what he had written. When working with his therapist, he often found it difficult to articulate exactly what he was experiencing at the moment. However, over the week he could process it all through writing. Then, when they came back together, the safety of having the concrete words on the page made it easier for him to communicate. Later on, when he had easier access to his own process and felt safer, he read the journal aloud less frequently. However, he continued to use it for himself.

RECORDING

Another tack you can take is to record your sessions and listen to them in the car or in the privacy of your home. This reexposure allows you not only to recall what you talked about, but to listen and process it more deeply or in a different way. Conversations in therapy are often highly emotionally charged. Often you won't be able to absorb it all the first time through. Also, sometimes we misconstrue what others say to us in sessions. By listening again we not only have the chance to receive the message more accurately, but we also can notice how we distorted it the first time around.

Our particular ways of distorting things are clues to the way we view and respond to the world.

Lois talked with her therapist Nathan about her latest interactions with her son Cody. She had great difficulty setting firm limits with Cody, in part because whenever she did, her husband took Cody's side. The night before, she'd allowed Cody to have the car keys, even though she had told him he was forbidden to drive because he had violated curfew the previous weekend. He convinced her that he needed the car to go to work, as the bus took a very indirect route, tripling the time to and from his job.

Nathan began to explore with Lois what happened when she and Cody got into this type of dialogue. Lois began to defend both Cody and her decision to give him the keys, even though Lois had begun the conversation by expressing frustration with her own decision.

When Lois listened to the tape of the session while driving home, she noticed that Nathan had said how challenging it would be for anyone in her position to stand firm. She didn't remember hearing that at all. Suddenly Lois realized that she was defending herself because she assumed Nathan thought her weak for backing down. Furthermore, she thought Nathan was telling her that she'd done it wrong. She also realized that, rather than making a judgment regarding her decision, Nathan had tried to understand with her what went into it. He wanted her to decide how she felt about it, not to blame her for it.

She had blocked out his support for her and his genuine curiosity about how she had made her decision. She also saw how she expected others to second-guess her decisions. Her husband often did this, and she often did it to herself.

This insight opened the door for her to explore with Nathan whether she might easily hear others' comments as critical and miss their support.

Couples or families can also benefit from recording, either during or between sessions. We often are not aware of how we talk to one another. Recording our conversations and listening to them, either alone or together, gives us a way to hear ourselves and learn more about our impact on others. You can also use recording as a way to bring information into the therapy session.

ARTWORK

Some may prefer a nonverbal method, such as visual arts or music, for working with what comes up in the process of therapy.

In their work together, Johannah and her therapist talked about ways in which she had protected herself from an abusive stepmother. She came back the next session with two pictures she'd drawn that showed her relationship to the protection. In the first, she was surrounded by a concrete wall, itself protected by barbed wire. In the second, she was wrapped in a beautiful blanket that both protected and nurtured her, yet could easily be removed when she was ready to connect with the world.

READING

Many therapists suggest reading. The fact that you're reading this book indicates that this could be a good avenue for you.

It's highly likely that someone has written about whatever you're dealing with. Reading is helpful because it helps you see that you're not alone. In a similar way, many people find help from movies, plays, or TV shows. It can be extremely affirming to read or hear about others who have had experiences similar to yours. It also gives you new ways of thinking about your own situation. In the back of this book is a list of books that clients and therapists have found useful.

Experiments

Another helpful type of homework is to experiment with acting in a way that isn't your usual way of doing things, and seeing how others react, how it feels, and what thoughts occur to you while doing it. Some therapists suggest specific experiments for couples. A technique called "caring days"[3] calls for each partner to take a day to show caring in the way the other person wants to receive it. This approach helps each partner see what the other actually wants and values. Sometimes couples write down positive behaviors they have tried or that they noticed in each other between sessions. A therapist may suggest that they not tell one another what they've written until they return to the next session, so they can focus more on their internal reactions, rather than on what they hope to gain from their partners.

What if Homework Doesn't Work?

All of the suggestions in this chapter require some action and effort on your part. None of the suggestions is perfect, and none works for absolutely everyone. If something doesn't work for you, maybe you aren't ready to take that kind of action yet. It may seem too threatening. If so, it may help to practice it with your therapist before trying it out on your own. It might seem more doable if you have the company of someone who supports you.

My client Merryl was extremely competent, had a responsible, well-paying job, and was not in debt. However, she was sure that she was in danger of getting a letter stating that she had made a terrible mistake and owed a huge payment. She was so afraid that she avoided opening her mail for weeks, letting it pile up at the door. After several sessions, she came up with a stopgap plan. She would take the pile, throw it all in a box, and send it to an accountant, whom she paid to sort her mail, pay her bills, and balance her checkbook. After several months of this, she decided she wanted to face her anxiety more directly.

We began a course of treatment that we called Mailbox Therapy.

Merryl began bringing the contents of her box to each session. We looked through the mail together. Although she still sent the bills to her accountant, with my support, she was able to sort through everything, eliminating the junk mail and actually reading the bills herself.

Then the inevitable happened. One day she found a doctor's bill that she thought had been covered by insurance. She became very agitated; her breath was shallow and her heart raced. I encouraged her to relax into her chair and breathe deeply, and we rehearsed a phone call to the doctor's office to resolve the problem. She picked up the phone and made the call. She learned that she did indeed have to pay the bill and promised to put a check in the mail immediately. She now realized that even though her worst-case scenario had occurred, she was able to handle it. And, in time, the pile she brought into our sessions became smaller and smaller.

The mail, not surprisingly, was a metaphor for a bigger core belief with which Merryl struggled: that no matter how competent she appeared to be, in reality she was deeply flawed and would eventually be found out. As we sorted through the mail, as well as her feelings, we explored and challenged that core belief.

Some therapists may rarely or never make these kinds of concrete suggestions. Some might simply encourage you to think about what happened in a session or to notice your emotions, your internal reactions, and your actions. Although this doesn't sound particularly active, the results can be powerful. By simply raising our awareness of an issue, we can change our relationship to it.

Lots of clients don't think about their issues between sessions, and they may not even remember what occurred in earlier sessions. This doesn't mean that they aren't doing their work. Like Della above, who changed the way she parented her children, they may be working on a subconscious level.

On the other hand, it could mean that they are working on difficult material that is painful to keep in their conscious awareness. If you have trouble remembering the content of sessions, you can ask your therapist to help. In my experience, most therapists try to keep a record of their conversations with clients, and can remind you what you talked about previously, including any ideas either of you presented for where to take the conversation next.[4]

Although it might seem a bit creepy to think that someone is keeping a written record of your most personal information, it can also be a source of comfort. It is, after all, a record of your story—a record that you have the legal right to see. It is both the story you brought to therapy and the story you and your therapist created together during your work. And it can feel good to know that your therapist holds the memory of what you've been doing together.

OTHER THINGS YOU CAN DO TO ENHANCE YOUR THERAPY

You or your therapist might decide that there are other things you can do that will help your therapeutic process, such as self-help and support groups, alternative healing approaches, and medication.

SELF-HELP AND SUPPORT GROUPS

Therapists frequently refer clients to self-help groups. The most well known are the 12-step groups based on the principles of Alcoholics Anonymous. There are 12-step groups for many types of addictive behavior, as well as for those who have family members suffering from an addiction. These groups do not have a leader, but they do have a very specific structure for each meeting and a clear set of guidelines for participation. For example, people are expected not to give advice or to analyze the behavior of others in the group. Typically these groups are open-ended, with no official start or end date. Everyone is welcome and there is no charge. People often like to find a group where they feel comfortable and then attend that group regularly; however, unlike in therapy groups, regular attendance is not required. Like group therapy, these groups give people the opportunity to learn and get support from others who are dealing with similar challenges.

Unlike self-help groups, support groups do usually have a trained leader and nearly all focus on a particular topic. For example, you might attend a parenting group, a grief group for people who have suffered the loss of a significant other, or a group for people who have been diagnosed with cancer. These groups differ from therapy groups in that they generally have an educational component. For example, the facilitator of a parenting group might spend a portion of the meeting teaching limit-setting skills. Although people talk about their challenges and get help on the central issue, participants are generally not encouraged to work on deeper therapeutic issues. Many support groups are time limited; others are open-ended and ongoing.

Alternative Healing

The possibilities regarding alternative healing approaches are numerous, but I will mention just a few. Some therapists recommend meditation and yoga as ways to get more deeply in touch with how your body and mind work, and to live *in* your experience rather than trying to avoid it. Others say that therapeutic massage, dance therapy, or another form of bodywork can be used to access the limbic feelings we store in our bodies.

Medication

Your therapist might also suggest that you consider taking psychotropic (brain-centered) medication. These medicines have an effect on mood and thought processes. Unless your therapist is a doctor or a nurse (or, in some states, a psychologist), he can't prescribe such medications himself, but he can refer you to a specialist who can. Although many people obtain such prescriptions from their general practitioners, it's best, if possible, to find a psychiatrist or a nurse or psychologist with specific training in psychotropic medications.

If your therapist suggests medication, it's wise to learn all you can about what type of medication is being prescribed, what its possible side effects might be, and how long you can expect to take it. The person who gives you the prescription should be able to answer these questions. In addition, it's worth finding out how your medication works, from the points of view of both those who prescribe it and those who take it. *Clinical Psychopharmacology Made Ridiculously Simple*, by John Preston and James Johnston,[5] is a very basic text that will give you good information about the use of these medications. It's written for physicians, but clients have also found it useful and easy to read. You also might find that people's descriptions of their own experiences with taking the medication (for example, in autobiographies or Internet chat rooms) are useful resources.

When you meet with a doctor or nurse, be sure to explain all the symptoms you are experiencing. It's also important that you give written permission for this person to speak with your therapist. That way, they can share important information with each other about their work with you, so that you get the best possible help. Most likely you'll see the doctor or nurse a few times at first once you begin taking medication, so she can determine whether the medicine is working, whether the dosage is correct, and whether there are any problems. After that, you'll probably see her only occasionally, perhaps once or twice a year, to check in and renew (or eventually discontinue) your prescription. Make sure that you follow any directions regarding how long you should take the medication, how much you should take, and any precautions you should take. In addition, it's important to let your doctor or nurse know right away if you have any bothersome side effects, or if you feel the medicine isn't working. This information will help her figure out what you need.

For most people, the thought of having to take a medication is disturbing. Is it a sign of weakness? Should you "tough it out" rather than depend on a drug? Will you not be yourself anymore? Will you become addicted? Will you experience side effects? All of these concerns are reasonable. Often it takes much trial and error to figure out the type and amount of medication that's best for each particular person. Medication is neither a sure fix nor a completely safe solution.

However, there are many times when medication can be extremely helpful, even life saving. Most psychiatrists agree that medication is necessary for serious conditions such as schizophrenia, bipolar disorder, and major depression. For some people, medication can provide enough relief from a debilitating symptom to allow them to work more produc-tively in talk therapy. For example, if you are depressed, you may find yourself extremely tired, lacking the energy to do anything, much less the hard work of therapy. Or you may feel so anxious or worried that you can't sleep at night. The sleep deprivation, in combination with the anxiety, may im-pair your ability to think clearly. The right medication can get your brain chemistry back in balance, so that you can think more clearly and interact better with others.

All of the activities mentioned in this chapter can help you move through the stages of change. You will decide, with the help of your therapist, which, if any, are appropriate for you. As I have already said, as you progress, you'll likely discover that some themes recur in your life, themes that we call your "core issues." These can usually be traced back to our early experiences of anxiety, shame, and guilt, and how we have learned to cope with them. In the next chapter, we examine these three natural and universal human emotions.

CHAPTER 10

Core Issues

Anxiety, Shame, and Guilt 101

Over the years, I've given many clients what I call my introductory lectures: Anxiety 101, Shame 101, and Guilt 101. We encounter all of these emotions early in life, before the prefrontal cortex is fully developed, and we therefore absorb and understand them first with the limbic system. Understanding these emotions enhances your ability to consciously work with them. This is the first step to learning how to manage them rather than letting them control you.

ANXIETY 101

Anxiety, whether it manifests cognitively as worry or in physiological symptoms such as a racing heart, is a fear reaction to real or perceived danger. A mechanism in the brain alerts us to danger, sending us into a vigilant fight/flight/freeze mode so that we can protect ourselves.

Often anxiety shows up as a fear of real physical danger. There are genuinely dangerous people, animals, plants, microbes, and situations in the world. There is always something that a reasonable person can fear, and being aware of danger is a good thing. It alerts us to do what we can to protect ourselves. Lock the doors. Wash your hands. Bring rain gear and a flashlight when you go on a hike. Drive carefully. Watch where and with whom you walk at night.

Sometimes we are anxious about interpersonal consequences. We might worry that someone will be angry or hurt or disappointed in us, and that this will cause them or us terrible distress, perhaps damaging or even ending our relationship. We might also be anxious that we won't meet our expectations for ourselves. Perhaps we're afraid that we'll make a mistake, or that we'll miss something important, or that we'll fail some sort of test. And sometimes we fear physical or emotional pain.

WHERE DOES ANXIETY START?

Erik Erikson, a well-known psychologist, proposed a model that describes the dilemmas people face at each stage of human development. He did not assume that people completely resolve the conflicts presented at each stage, but that, ideally, they would fall more on the positive than the negative side of each duality.

He named the first stage "trust versus mistrust." The question is whether an infant experiences the world as a safe place. Will his needs for physical and emotional nurturing and care, *in general*, be met? The emphasis on "in general" is important, because none of us can count on others to meet our every need. A baby gets hungry and her mother can't feed her right away. Or perhaps the baby is fussy and her father can't quite figure out what's causing her unhappiness or discomfort. Even the most attentive parent can't be tuned in and accurate all of the time. In fact, that's a good thing.

It creates those moments of stress that encourage brain growth. Assuming the baby has a basic sense that the world is trustworthy, she will learn to use the times when the world doesn't come through for her to gain the ability to come through for (or soothe) herself—for example, by sucking her thumb or snuggling with a stuffed animal. As we grow, we learn that we can count on others and on ourselves—not always, but enough.

However, our very survival depends on the world being fundamentally safe. Infants and young children are totally dependent on those who care for them to provide that safety. If a caretaker severely neglects or abuses his child, the child could die. This is possible even if the neglect or abuse isn't physically threatening, because of the fact that infants and young children require emotional attachment in addition to basic physical care to thrive. The abused or neglected child almost always suffers severe psychological impairment, including having great difficulty trusting the world.

As we saw in Chapter Three, the primary function of the limbic system is to ensure survival. However, the mere perception of a threat to the infant's survival will be registered in the limbic system just as surely as an actual threat. On that deepest level, a limbic memory of a mother who was inattentive when we were hungry, seemed not to keep us safe, scared us when she was angry, or who actually abused or neglected us can all evoke the same core fear with the same power. As a result, even as adults, we all have, still stored in our limbic brain, at least a trace of this fundamental fear of death by abandonment (neglect) or annihilation (abuse). When we feel vulnerable we are driven, to some extent, by this very raw and completely human emotion.

Anxiety-Based Living

Some of us are more driven by fear than others. If you regularly experience danger, the brain's alert mechanism can get stuck in danger mode, triggering an anxious response to almost any situation, whether or not it is really dangerous. In addition, some people are born with a temperament that is especially sensitive to cues of danger and are more anxious and vigilant than those with a different temperament.

Often people respond to a high level of anxiety by putting an inordinate amount of energy into organizing their life around trying to avoid or respond to it. I call this taking an *anxiety-based* approach to life.[1]

Anxiety Avoidance Strategies

We all develop ways of managing our lives. But our management or coping style itself becomes a problem when our particular strategy gets in our way and we feel we have no other useful options. Since we all have some degree of anxiety, we all have strategies, such as the ones described below. However, when our lives are anxiety-based, we use these strategies far beyond when they are useful.

Anxiety Avoidance Strategy #1: Defenses

Although the word has a bad connotation—no one likes to be called defensive—defenses can be very useful for dealing with life's challenges. I introduced the defenses of denial and rationalization earlier, in the example of Jake, who was very overweight and had dangerously high blood pressure and a far-too-rapid heart rate.

Like all coping mechanisms, denial can be an appropriate response. Elizabeth Kubler-Ross, well known for her work on the process of grieving, noted that denial is often a first response to hearing difficult news. It's a way to protect ourselves from the trauma of what we are hearing until we can let it in and integrate it. However, if you stay in denial and don't move to the final stage of acceptance, you will fail to come to terms with the loss or impending loss.[2]

Like denial, rationalization can keep a painful reality at bay until we are better able to deal with it. If we use it temporarily, and later face whatever it is more squarely, it sometimes gives us necessary space.

Remember Paul, whose wife Sema betrayed him by kissing and fondling other men when she was drunk? Her explanation—that she did it because she'd had too much to drink—is a form of rationalization. Paul was also engaging in rationalization by accepting the explanation and by assuming, when he first entered therapy, that the problem was primarily his insecurity about the marriage. Yet neither of them even considered the possibility that her drinking itself was a problem. This is an example of denial. Paul and Sema used both of these defenses to avoid facing their anxiety that Sema's behavior might destroy their relationship.

Anxiety Avoidance Strategy #2: Make No Decisions

Some people avoid decision making because they are afraid of the consequences of committing to any given direction. Roseanna disliked her unchallenging job but was afraid no one would offer her a better one or that she would find herself trapped in an even worse one. Alphie had the same feeling about dating. He felt very lonely and wanted a partner, but he was sure that no one he wanted would want him, or that he would quickly get stuck in another destructive relationship. Any road Roseanna or Alphie took was fraught with potential danger. They believed that they could avoid anxiety by doing nothing, but that "strategy" led to boredom for Roseanna and loneliness for Alphie. They both rejected any suggestion that the danger they feared might not occur, or if it did, that they could find ways to handle it. Each gave a "yes—but" response—a convincing argument for why changing was wrong or wouldn't work.

Anxiety Avoidance Strategy #3: Control

Many people who try to control what others do are scared of the real or imagined consequences of not controlling them. Jerome always wanted his wife Pat nearby whenever he was home, even sitting with him to watch TV when she wasn't interested in the program. When Pat went back to work after their kids started high school, Jerome was unhappy about her decision. When she came home later than usual one night, he became angry, giving her the third degree about where she'd been and what she'd done. When Jerome finally agreed to join Pat in therapy, they learned that underneath Jerome's controlling behavior was a fear that he would lose Pat. He was terrified of being alone; having Pat nearby and under his control kept his terror at bay.

Anxiety Avoidance Strategy # 4: Engaging in Mood-Altering Behaviors

Use of drugs, alcohol, gambling, food, or other activities or substances to alter one's mood is another common strategy for avoiding, or masking, anxiety or other pain. None of these activities, in moderation, is necessarily problematic. However, when use becomes abuse or addiction, the consequences can be severe, ranging from lost money, to betrayal of family and friends, to physical illness, to death.

The best definition for chemical dependency I know is that the chemically dependent person is searching for a reward by engaging in a pathological relationship with a mood-altering substance. The expected *reward* is pleasure or, at least, less pain. The addiction is a *relationship* because the person organizes his life to accommodate it. The relationship is *pathological* because the activity actually causes more pain in the long run, and often, in the short run as well. As you've probably heard, denial often accompanies addiction, making it difficult to recognize. If you are strongly committed to an addiction, you are not consciously aware of the pain it is causing you and others.

Solutions for Dealing with Anxiety: Learning to Tolerate It

Avoiding anxiety, although it may offer temporary relief, is not ultimately effective. Anxiety is part of the human condition, a given in everyone's life. And because anxiety alerts us to real danger, if you overuse strategies for avoiding it, you risk experiencing worse pain than the pain you were hoping to escape.

Furthermore, we cannot avoid the ultimate losses about which we are anxious. Life is impermanent and unpredictable. Couples break up. Friends move. Family members die. Bridges and stock markets collapse. The only thing we can ever be sure about is that everything will not be okay. Life never turns out *just* the way we want it to.

So, you have two choices. You can close yourself off to life and thereby live in a constant state of loss. Or you can engage in your life more fully, acting out of your best and most honest intentions, knowing that, although you will ultimately lose whomever or whatever you love, the love itself is nourishing. Learning to tolerate the inevitable anxiety is key to our ability to live life fully.

Many thinkers suggest that the antidote for anxiety is a spiritual one. Recall that anxiety is born out of the trust versus mistrust dilemma. Here therapeutic and spiritual questions overlap. Can you trust that some force bigger than you is reliable? Can you trust that you yourself are reliable? One common idea is that our perception of God, or a source of power that resides in and is greater than us, upon which we can rely for strength and care, comes initially from our parents. Those who propose this concept are not referring to the fact that parents teach us what they believe about religion and spirituality. They are suggesting that when we are babies, our parents embody that higher power. Our experience of our parents as nurturing or abusive, safe or dangerous, reliable or unreliable, shapes our experience of the universe. When we are adequately cared for, we internalize, at least to some extent, the ability to take care of ourselves; when we are not, we tend to feel lost and afraid in the world until we learn self-care in another way.

Successful dealing with anxiety requires looking it in the eye and learning that we can live with it and tolerate its discomfort. In facing both life and death, we can trust whatever is divine in ourselves and in the universe to help us live in the midst of life's challenges.

Remember Elizabeth, whose change in her relationship with the church's teachings caused a painful disruption of the status quo in her relationships with her husband and sons? She initially resisted acknowledging the change even to herself, much less to others, but eventually found she could no longer do that. As she faced and dealt with the changes, she found that the very spiritual path she was afraid to take was also helping her. It enabled her to trust that she and her family were part of a larger reality, one that would help them all ride life's waves and cope with whatever emerged.

GETTING HELP WITH ANXIETY
FROM YOUR THERAPIST

Your therapist can help you with anxiety in various ways:

- First, by being a trustworthy person, she can help you experience that primary sense that you can rely on something larger than you—in this case, your healing relationship.
- Second, she can help you learn about how you can trust your own capacities. This might include challenging you to think through your worst-case scenarios and figure out how you would manage them.
- Third, she can recommend other resources, such as meditation, yoga, or a faith tradition that speaks to you, all of which can increase your ability to connect to a larger source of wisdom.
- Fourth, she can recommend that you consider psychotropic medicine, which can help if your anxiety is overwhelming or impeding your ability to function.

SHAME 101

Although we all know the word *shame*, and all of us have experienced it, it's a phenomenon that many people don't quite
understand. When we feel shame, we feel bad about who we
are. Like anxiety, shame (and its cousin, guilt) are not only
universal, but serve a useful purpose.

WHERE DOES SHAME START?

Erikson's second stage of development, beginning at around
2 years old, is called "autonomy vs. shame and doubt." Children entering this stage are starting to notice that they are
separate from their parents. Anyone who's had a toddler
knows about the Terrible Twos, so named because the child's
favorite word is some version of "no." And, in response,
that's also the parent's most commonly used word. The child
says, in essence, "I'm not sure who I am, but I'm getting the
picture that I'm not you." The parent's job is to give the
child opportunities to learn who she is, while, at the same
time, setting appropriate limits.

I discovered when raising my own children what a hard
job this is. You're supposed to let the children be themselves
and also show them the way, sometimes both at once. Somehow you need to discern when to do which one.

The child's work at this stage is to begin to figure out who
he is. If the message he gets is that he is bad, the child feels
ashamed. Because the child is very young, his prefrontal cortex is still almost entirely undeveloped. As with fear and
anxiety, he experiences the shame in his limbic system. Also
as with fear and anxiety, there's no way for a human being to
avoid it.

In fact, as I've often said to clients, those who never feel shame (or guilt) don't care at all about what society or others expect of them or what impact they have on others. They are truly dangerous. If I malevolently hurt someone, I *should* feel shame. If I don't, there's something terribly wrong.

My colleague Thad runs a group for men who have battered their partners. One of the assignments in the group is for each man to talk in detail about the most violent thing he ever did. The men commonly use denial and rationalization to avoid facing the consequences of their behavior, thus allowing them to continue it. Thad tries to break through those defenses to help them really see these consequences and feel their impact. He says that when they do this they feel bad about themselves—they feel ashamed. That shame helps them get in touch with the seriousness of their behavior—a necessary awareness if they are to take full responsibility for it.

Shame-Based Living

However, many of us experience more shame than is useful. This can happen if you get a strong message from your parents or caretakers that you are unacceptable or bad.

When children are neglected or abused, they usually experience a strong sense of shame. Sometimes caretakers are not able to tolerate any of a child's characteristics or behaviors that are different from their own, or from their idea of who the child should be. Children respond to such intolerance by feeling ashamed. Sometimes caretakers themselves feel a great deal of shame and pass it on as if through osmosis. If I believe I'm bad, it's hard not to give the message to my child that she's bad, too. Sometimes shame is passed down through the generations. Whole families may feel shame about who they are, sometimes in part because they belong to a cultural or ethnic group that has experienced a lot of shame.

Shame is a very powerful feeling, and it is typically accompanied by a serious cognitive distortion. For example, a person experiencing what I call a *shame attack* may think something like, "Every positive thing I ever thought about myself was false. The truth is, I am basically a bad person." This distortion occurs because when we are in shame, we are not firing on all six cylinders—that is, not using our prefrontal cortex. Maybe we will in a few minutes, or a few days, or a few months. But at the moment, we can't think clearly about ourselves.

STRATEGIES FOR AVOIDING SHAME

As with anxiety, many people develop ways of responding to shame that are counterproductive. The more *shame-based* your life is, the more time you spend either feeling shame or trying to avoid the feeling. Defenses such as denial and rationalization are attempts to avoid feeling it. Other strategies that people use specifically to avoid feeling shame include the following.

Shame Avoidance Strategy #1: Hiding

Hiding means keeping information about yourself from others that you think says something bad about you. It may be an experience you've had, like having been sexually abused. Or perhaps it's a feeling, such as anger, that you believe is dangerous and shouldn't be exposed.

Josephine is a very kind and accepting person whom others greatly respect. Like anyone, she is critical of others at times, but she considers this criticalness a deep personality flaw. She goes out of her way to keep those thoughts and feelings from surfacing, apologizing if she ever says something that may reveal them. But she feels very insecure in her friendships. She is afraid that her friends will discover what a bad person she is if she criticizes them or even talks about someone else in a critical manner. Then, she is convinced, they will abandon her.

Shame Avoidance Strategy #2: Amputation

Some people try to cut out the aspect of themselves that causes them to feel ashamed. People who use this strategy typically respond to feedback about a personal flaw with a comment such as "Okay, now that I see this about myself, how do I change—that is, get rid of it quickly?" The goal of amputation is to escape the shame as fast as possible. This approach often causes people to jump into action before they are really ready. As a result, the action backfires.

Recall Laticia, who had a tendency to confess in order to avoid criticism. If someone was upset with her, she felt very ashamed. By confessing her faults to that person and seeking his or her forgiveness, she hoped to relieve her shame. As we learned, this strategy often backfired. Sometimes her apologies just made others angrier with her because they felt manipulated into reassuring her. And sometimes she made herself vulnerable to others who used the information to hurt her.

Shame Avoidance Strategy #3: Perfectionism

Perfectionism can take many forms, depending on a person's values. Maybe it means being a straight-A student.

Maybe it means doing everything you can to be a good daughter, husband, or parent. Maybe it means always being nice. Whatever it is, you are working hard to deny any part of yourself that is imperfect and therefore worthy of shame. The problem with this approach is that you will eventually fail. No one can maintain perfection over time. Our human edges will stick out, shattering the image.

Steve thought he not only had to hide the fact that he had chronic fatigue, but also had to do the work of three people. Although his disability worsened because of too much stress, he persisted in taking on more obligations than even a physically healthy person would be able to sustain. He was very successful at work and had a long-term relationship with Ken, as well as many good friends. However, he feared that any hint of weakness would prove him a fraud, just like his father, who was also successful but used his success to cover a multitude of problems, including having sexually abused both Steve and his sister. Steve fell into deep despair when he contracted a serious case of Lyme disease that forced him to cut back on his work.

Shame Avoidance Strategy #4:
"Take It Back"

This is an interactive form of shame avoidance that people use when someone has said something about them that evoked feelings of shame. The goal is to negate or at least minimize what the other person has said. Often people do this by shaming back.

Martha's family teased her a lot, ostensibly in fun, but often with a critical edge. Whenever she protested that their comments hurt her, they told her she was too sensitive. Often in families with much shame in the air, a person who is will-ing to name what is happening or challenge the unspoken agreements becomes the scapegoat, and may be labeled the crazy one.

Another form of shaming back is when a person responds to negative feedback by saying something like, "How can you hurt me like this?" The message here is, "I've done nothing. You are hurting me out of malice, not because you have something important to say about my impact on you. You should feel ashamed."

A final form of "take it back" is what I call *preemptive shame*. It's similar to "How can you hurt me like this?" but, rather than attacking someone else, it involves collapsing in a puddle of shame. This tactic delivers the message, "I'm so fragile that I can't bear to hear what you are saying," and it implies, "You're a bad person for making me feel so bad about myself."

Whenever Jerry would let his wife know that something upset him, she would apologize repeatedly, saying how terri-ble she felt. Jerry didn't want that much power. He just wanted her to hear and accept his feelings, and to sometimes say, "I'm sorry." Eventually, he felt he couldn't express his feelings in the relationship because his wife felt so terrible about herself, no matter how gently he spoke.

SOLUTIONS FOR DEALING WITH SHAME: ACCEPTING OUR HUMANITY

Strategies aimed at avoiding, rather than dealing with, shame are not particularly effective. Dealing successfully with shame requires accepting and working with those parts of ourselves about which we feel ashamed. If you don't recognize the fact that there's a box of Kleenex sitting next to you, you can't do anything with it. You can't use it or offer it to someone. This is equally true for our internal realities. Anything we don't recognize can't be dealt with; it is outside our conscious sphere of influence.

GETTING HELP FOR SHAME FROM YOUR THERAPIST: COMPASSION AND ACCOUNTABILITY

Shame is both evoked and healed by interpersonal connections.[3] Finding the right person (or people) is the key to healing shame. Such a person has to be someone you trust in two very important ways. First, you have to trust her to have compassion for you and not to intentionally shame you. Second, you have to trust her to tell you the truth—to hold you, and help you hold yourself, accountable.

In order to reveal yourself to her, you need to believe that your therapist is in your corner. This means that you experience her as understanding and having compassion for how you came to experience things the way you do. "In your corner," however, doesn't mean always on your side. She might not always take your point of view. She might challenge you to look at other options for how to approach or understand something or someone. She might think you are hurting yourself or someone else more than you realize. This feedback helps you hold yourself accountable for the impact your feelings, thoughts, and behavior have on yourself and others.

Your therapist can be this type of person for you. In fact, she needs to be in order to help you.

Having both compassion and accountability is very important. One without the other is problematic. If someone has compassion for your pain without holding you account-able (or helping you hold yourself accountable), you may consider yourself a victim rather than someone who has the power to affect your own life. If someone holds you ac-countable without compassion, you may simply feel more ashamed of yourself.

When someone is compassionate *and* holds you account-able in your life, it gives you the room to begin to look at yourself, especially those parts of yourself that you are afraid to see clearly. This is what it means to feel safe with your therapist. You can begin to accept that certain parts of yourself exist and expand your choices for handling them. You don't rid yourself of these qualities. They are part of your humanity. Whatever they are, you came by them hon-estly. They are part of your temperament, and they were shaped by your environment and your personal response to that environment. They were your best efforts to handle whatever challenges life has presented you with. But they don't have to put limits on your growth.

When Paul and Sema, the couple who used denial and ra-tionalization to avoid their anxiety about Sema's drinking and sexual betrayal, finally started couples therapy, their therapist Adele could see that both of them felt intense shame. Paul moved between feeling ashamed of himself for his insecurity about his marriage despite Sema's reas-surances, and ashamed for being the type of person whose wife would betray him. Sema was ashamed that she was the type of person who would betray her husband. First, Adele acknowledged the difficulty of their situation and how much pain they both were feeling. Second, she did not accept their explanation of why Sema was sexually inappropriate with other men, or their unwillingness to look at the problems associated with Sema's drinking. She gently let them know that she thought there was more to all this than met the eye.

As they explored the situation, it became clear that Sema had come by her issues honestly. Sema's sexual behavior was driven in part by a fear of commitment. She had watched her mother suffer the consequences of two abusive marriages, and Sema herself had had several relationships with men who had cheated on her. Part of her was worried that if she really opened herself to Paul, he would abuse or betray her as well. Making out with other men helped her keep her distance—and kept Paul scared that he might lose her, so that he'd stay on his best behavior and not hurt her. But she also saw that she was treating Paul as abusively as she had been treated in the past. And she realized he might actually leave if she kept it up.

It also became clear that many members of Sema's family drank heavily. This looked normal to her. And her drinking masked painful feelings, just as it had for her mother. Although the mask worked temporarily, it certainly couldn't keep the emotions from affecting her. She acted in response to these emotions without conscious awareness of their impact. The additional shame about betraying Paul, which she attributed to her drinking, exacerbated the pain she was trying to escape.

Paul also came honestly by his willingness to accept Sema's hurtful treatment of him. As they explored his history, they learned that he had always felt unlovable as a child. His older brother and younger sister were the family stars, very popular in school, and got all of the attention from their parents.

In contrast, Paul felt like a loser. Girls never wanted to go out with him and he had few friends. Although he was a decent student, he never got the top grades or any awards for high achievement, as his siblings did.

That Sema was attracted to him surprised him. He never expected to marry such a wonderful woman. Refusing to accept her explanation would have meant either facing the perceived "truth" that he wasn't really worthy of her attention or, perhaps worse, facing the "truth" that there was something wrong with Sema, whom he idolized.

With regard to the drinking, it turned out that Paul's maternal grandparents drank heavily—his grandfather would pass out at family events—though no one in the family ever acknowledged any problem. Until Paul, in the course of his own therapy, asked his mother about it, she had never talked about how ashamed she felt as a child when her parents were drunk. Like Paul, she had few friends, in part because she was afraid to invite anyone over to the house. She had also considered herself a loser. Paul thus inherited the family shame and denial. This explained more about why he was willing to allow himself to be hurt repeatedly. Although he didn't recognize it, he felt he deserved it.

Adele's response to the couple, which combined both compassion and accountability, allowed them to face their pain and to look at their behavior with compassion for themselves and for each other. It also helped them face how their behavior had exacerbated, rather than healed the pain. For the first time, they spoke more honestly about themselves to each other and began to make a firmer, more intimate connection with, and commitment to, one another.

Looking at and facing the things that make you feel ashamed does not mean that you can dig them all out and fix them. Paul and Sema both continued to hit moments of shame, occasionally and temporarily reverting to their old ways of managing it. Sema didn't betray Paul anymore, but sometimes when she was upset with Paul, she would comment about her attraction to other men rather than talk about what was bothering her. And rather than tell her how he felt about this, Paul might try to explain it away, telling himself that his own feelings of insecurity didn't matter. However, in therapy they learned to identify much more quickly what was going on and talk more productively with each other.

Greater awareness and understanding help us get better at managing our emotional lives. As you talk with your therapist, you can begin to see that your shame is only a part of your reality. You can look at yourself with a larger vision and see yourself with greater compassion. As this happens, you gain more courage to change. You begin to move from contemplation to action.

GUILT 101

Guilt is the feeling we get when we've done something we think we shouldn't have, or neglected to do something we think we should have. Guilt and shame often occur at the same time, but by itself, guilt is a less powerful feeling. "I feel bad because I did that" (an expression of guilt) carries less punch than "I feel bad about myself because I did that" (an expression of shame). Both guilt and shame often evoke anxiety because *doing* something bad (guilt) or *being* bad (shame) are potentially dangerous. We risk punishment in the form of abandonment, abuse, or both.

WHERE DOES GUILT START?

Erikson's third stage of development is "initiative vs. guilt." In this stage, the child is learning how to do things. Often you'll see children imitating what their parents do, perhaps working alongside them. This is also the time when they begin to learn lots of skills—from riding a tricycle, to playing an instrument, to making a peanut butter sandwich. It's a time when they start to take the lead in their lives, deciding what challenges they will take on—hence the term *initiative.*

This stage begins when the child is about 3 years old, at which point the prefrontal cortex is beginning, slowly, to take shape. Feeling guilty requires conscious awareness (that is, use of the prefrontal cortex) of both what you are doing and whether it's acceptable behavior. By contrast, anxiety and shame can occur solely as feelings, without any words or thinking attached to them.

Naturally, some of the things children decide to try are not in their own best interest. A 4-year-old might ride his tricycle into a busy street. A 10-year-old might make a huge mess in the living room and then leave it for someone else to pick up. Parents must help children become aware of what they've done, often stopping or redirecting them. We want children to learn to be responsible. We want them to know when what they are doing is wrong or dangerous. The parent's job at this point is to help children begin to develop the prefrontal cortex skill of exercising good judgment. The feeling of guilt is a signal that we are doing or considering

doing something that is deemed wrong. Guilt helps us monitor our own behavior in a positive way.

Guilt-Based Living

Many people feel more guilt than is useful, however. They
find themselves making decisions simply to avoid feeling
guilty, usually because they lack any other internal compass
by which to recognize right or wrong. Their lives become
guilt-based. This perspective can take hold if their families
had an overabundance of very powerful rules about how
they should behave, especially when those rules are accompanied by the message, "If you don't behave properly, you
will no longer belong."

Some families, as well as some closely knit communities,
share the characteristic that if you agree with their values and
premises, you are warmly welcomed, but the boundaries for
who's in and who's out are tightly drawn, and if you don't
closely toe the line, you're out.

Tim's family, with whom he had been very close, dis-
owned him when he told them he was gay. They considered
his behavior a sin and firmly believed that this core aspect of
his sexuality was deeply wrong. Ari's family rejected him
and his new wife, who was not of their Jewish faith. His
very traditional grandparents even "sat shiva" for him, a ritual normally performed when a family member dies. Josh
grew up in a radical left-wing family, where only liberal politics were acceptable. Whenever he challenged the family's
party line, his siblings labeled him "brainwashed," "intoler-
ant," and sometimes even "racist," refusing to converse with
him about politics at all.

All families have spoken and unspoken rules regarding how family members treat one another. Often those rules include taking care of one or more individuals' feelings. Of course, it's good to consider others' feelings when deciding what to do, and generally to make decisions that do not harm others. That's part of behaving responsibly in relationship to others. However, some people use that fundamental truth in a manipulative way.

After Eleana's parents were divorced, she lived with her grandparents. Her father lived in another state and her mother, whom she saw infrequently, had trouble with drugs. Whenever Eleana decided to spend time with her friends rather than with her mother, even when her mother was stoned or socializing with men who made Eleana feel creepy, her mother was very hurt, and she told Eleana so. As a result, Eleana felt a good deal of distance between herself and her mom—and felt that she herself was to blame for it. Somehow she was neglecting her mother.

Tim broke his family's spoken rule that to be okay you have to be heterosexual; Ari, the rule that you have to marry within the faith; and Josh, the rule that only certain political views are acceptable. Eleana broke the unspoken rule that it was her job to take care of her mother's feelings.

Tim's, Ari's Josh's, and Eleana's stories illustrate an important aspect of guilt. Whenever you break a rule, especially a powerful one, in your family or community, you will feel at least a little guilty. This is true even if the rule is clearly an unhealthy or unreasonable one. It comes with the territory. The guilt can cause confusion because we usually assume that if we have these feelings, we are doing something wrong. The confusion keeps a lot of people stuck in positions where they might not act in their own best interests—or, paradoxically, in others' best interests.

Harold has always played the role of family caretaker and lives according to a strong rule that this is his primary job. His brother Vick was evicted from his apartment, had little money, and was out of a job. In the past, Harold helped him out, both financially and by letting him stay with him, but Vick's problems kept recurring.

Harold and his wife were successful and stable, with plenty of money and an extra bedroom. However, his wife resented Vick's intrusion and irresponsible behavior, and worried about Vick's influence on their two children. She was angry at Harold for considering taking him in yet again. In addition, although Harold loved his brother, he was angry about the pressure from him and their parents, who had no resources of their own, to take care of him. He was also concerned that it would be detrimental to rescue Vick yet again. On the other hand, he worried that Vick would end up homeless and in deep trouble, maybe even with the law. He felt like a bad brother for refusing him a hand, especially when his own life was going so well.

Bao was a Hmong woman whose husband had a serious gambling problem. He not only spent all the family's money but often disappeared for weeks at a time on gambling sprees. When Bao tried to talk with him about it, he became very angry, threatening to hurt her and the children. Because he was unwilling to face and deal with the problem, Bao felt she had to leave, for her sake as well as for the sake of their children. She also fought for custody of the children in order to protect them, even though, in her Hmong culture, children traditionally stay with the father in the event of divorce. She felt both guilty and ashamed, as her husband and his family blamed her not only for leaving him in his time of need, but for taking the children with her and "betraying" the entire family by divorcing. She was breaking a huge rule: Family loyalty and togetherness trump everything. Bao believed she had made the right decision. But this didn't stop her from struggling with the self-doubt that always accompanies guilt.

Guilt Avoidance Strategies

People also use defenses to avoid guilt. However, because guilt requires the use of the prefrontal cortex, the strategies for dealing with it require using that part of the brain as well. Therefore, denial by itself doesn't work. Rationalization, on the other hand, can be quite effective. Sometimes we can, at least temporarily, talk ourselves out of feeling guilty about breaking a rule by telling ourselves why it's okay to do so.

There is only one strategy specifically designed for avoiding guilt: Obey all the rules. Like the other avoidance strategies we've discussed, this one has problems. First, it's almost impossible because most sets of rules have built-in contradictions. For example, if Harold followed the rule about being a good brother, he would break the one about being a good husband and father.

In addition, a rule might not be a good one to honor. Although breaking a rule has consequences, honoring it may cause you or others even greater pain. Harold's and Bao's stories above are both good examples of this point. If Harold were to break the rules about being a good brother and family caretaker, he would risk not only anger from his family, but the possibility that his brother would end up in more trouble. However, obeying the rule risked not only disruption in his own family—and danger to his children—but possibly doing his brother more harm by continuing to enable his irresponsible behavior.

Because she was breaking both a cultural and a family rule, Bao risked her husband's family's anger and blame as well as the rejection of her and her children by many in the larger community. However, obeying the rule that she should stay in the marriage, no matter what happened, put her and her children in potential financial and physical danger.

GETTING HELP WITH GUILT
FROM YOUR THERAPIST

In therapy you can get help in identifying and examining these rules. If by breaking a rule you inevitably feel guilt, and possibly shame and anxiety, you can't just assume that those feelings, by themselves, are an accurate monitor of what you should do. You only know for sure that they sound an alarm. They tell you you're breaking a rule. You need your prefrontal cortex to help you determine whether the rule is a good one—that is, one that is life-giving and that promotes respectful and loving connections between good-hearted people. If not, it may be a good rule to break.

As Bao's and Harold's stories suggest, this isn't an easy decision to make. Sometimes you have to decide between two difficult choices, each with serious consequences. Often it's difficult to determine whether you are rationalizing or actually making a good decision. However, if your therapist both holds you accountable and treats you with compassion, he can help you look closely at your decision to follow or break a rule, and this can help you make the decision with as much integrity as possible.

Like other developmental models, Erikson's stages represent a linear progression—trust versus mistrust begins in infancy, shame versus autonomy in toddlerhood, and initiative versus guilt at about 3. However, as the stories in this chapter suggest, the core issues connected with each stage not only interact with each other but also follow us through our lives, especially if we have families that reinforce them. Caretakers who use guilt and shame as forms of manipulation aren't likely to stop just because a child gets older. Furthermore, as we grow, new experiences present opportunities to revisit the core dilemmas.

For example, one of Erikson's later life stages is intimacy versus isolation. Being in an intimate relationship frequently, if not always, raises questions about trust, shame, and guilt. Being in an intimate relationship requires that you take the risk to open your heart and to trust that your partner won't hurt you when you are unprotected. This includes exposing parts of yourself about which you feel ashamed. Your partner needs to do the same. Taking these risks and exposing ourselves in this manner is difficult, and all of us at times resort to strategies designed to protect ourselves. As Paul's and Sema's stories illustrate, when one partner acts out of anxiety and shame, his or her behavior often evokes those feelings in the other. Guilt comes into the picture because each partner brings to the relationship a set of rules for what is acceptable behavior. Because it's impossible to share all of the same rules, you will inevitably break some of your partner's rules, either intentionally or unintentionally. This rule breaking becomes more complex when your partner experiences your rule breaking as a sign that you don't care about him or her or the relationship—an experience that evokes anxiety and perhaps shame.

The quality of your relationship with your therapist makes a significant difference in how successfully you use therapy to work with your core issues. Because of the phenomenon of transference—the tendency to see others through the lens of our prior experiences—your relationship with your therapist often evokes reactions related to those issues and offers you opportunities to work with them. In the next two chapters, we explore the relationship in more depth, looking specifically at the dynamics of safety and trust, power, and authority.

CHAPTER 11

Safety and Trust

As I stressed in Chapters Two and Three, both therapy and the development of the brain require an environment that is safe as well as challenging.

A safe relationship is necessary because success in therapy requires that the client be vulnerable. Initially, however, some people are reluctant to show emotional vulnerability because they believe that it is a sign of weakness. Others fear that if they express their emotions honestly, they will open a Pandora's box of negativity that could be harmful.

Morrie's father was alcoholic and emotionally and physically abusive to his wife and children. As a child, Morrie was afraid of his father's anger. When he began therapy, his therapist Shoshanna noticed that he avoided talking in depth about anything that bothered him. Instead, he would describe incidents that were already resolved—tied up in a pretty package. It was as if he were saying, "Well, I had this problem, but everything's fine now. I don't really need your help with it."

Shoshanna commented on this pattern, inviting Morrie to explore how it might have evolved. He began to recognize that underneath many of his stories was anger, a feeling he worked hard to deny or avoid. He told Shoshanna about an encounter he had had with his father some years earlier. Although largely estranged from his father for years after his parents divorced, Morrie lived in the same neighborhood as his dad. Morrie was planning to move to a different state, so he invited his father to a farewell dinner in a local restaurant. Throughout the meal, his father tried to get him to reconsider his plan to move. He wanted his son close by. Morrie explained that he had a wonderful job opportunity waiting for him, and that he hoped his father would be happy for him. But all his father said was, "Fine. Be selfish. It's nothing new."

Suddenly Morrie's anger at his father surged to the surface. He forgot he was in a public place and found himself standing up, pointing his finger, and screaming out his past hurt and betrayal.

His father, who had once been dangerous and larger than life, dissolved in tears. Morrie was horrified. Though he resented his father, he felt he had just done something unforgivable to the now elderly man. The incident confirmed Morrie's long held belief about how dangerous anger was— a belief he didn't even know he held. Morrie returned to his old habit, begun as a boy, of masking his feelings.

As he worked together with Shoshanna, Morrie became able, first, to tolerate the anxiety that his anger evoked and then to express whatever was bothering him in a constructive manner. He still didn't feel safe expressing his anger to people he was afraid he'd hurt. He needed to do it with someone whom he could trust not to be fearful, overwhelmed, or hurt by his anger. When he was able to trust Shoshanna to be that person, he was able to express his anger fully, and then to examine it, his fears about it, and the consequences of trying to mask or avoid it. He was also able to identify some strategies for facing and working with it. Eventually he was able to let himself be angry with people outside of the therapy office, and to express that anger honestly and constructively.

Trust Doesn't Just Happen

As Morrie's story suggests, trust in your therapist develops over time. Clients can't, and shouldn't, expect themselves to trust their therapists fully right away.

Alice didn't want to be in therapy. Her adult children insisted that she come to a family therapy session so they could confront her with what they remembered as her sexual abuse of them when they were young. She's blind in her right eye and used that fact to pretend she wasn't really sitting in a therapist's office. She purposely sat in a chair to the left of the therapist, Rhonda, so she couldn't see her. But she felt her. She noticed Rhonda moving closer to her when her kids expressed their rage at her. She heard Rhonda's warm tone. She sensed, on some level, that Rhonda would be safe. When she finally agreed to individual therapy to deal with her children's feedback, she chose to go to Rhonda.

Even though she had an initial good feeling about Rhonda, Alice wasn't about to tell her everything at once. She had to put it out, little by little, to see how Rhonda would react. Would she recoil in horror? Would she withdraw? Would she become angry or negatively judgmental? With each little step, Alice watched and saw that Rhonda consistently responded to her with with honesty and compassion.

As Alice began to trust Rhonda, she began to trust herself to handle what was inside. She remembered having been abused herself, something she had blocked from her mind for years. Several subsequent family therapy meetings with her children, as well as months of individual therapy, established that she hadn't sexually abused her children. Still, she began to see more clearly why her children saw her as they did. With Rhonda's help, she identified ways in which she had behaved that were intrusive, and that could easily be interpreted as abusive.

Because both of Alice's parents had sexually abused her, she had never learned appropriate boundaries or how to recognize when she felt violated herself. When she became a parent, she believed it was important to let her kids know that the body and sex are natural by being naked in front of her children and by taking no particular care to keep her and her husband's sexual activity private. Alice never noticed that the kids felt uncomfortable about this. As she began to acknowledge this, first to herself, and later to her children, she experienced a lot of shame about what she had done to her children, albeit unintentionally.

It took Alice a long time to accept Rhonda's compassion for her and to develop compassion for herself. During the first several months of therapy, only her pain about her family kept her going. She was highly motivated, but she was doing it for them. She couldn't imagine that she deserved to do it for herself, although Rhonda repeatedly let her know that she did. It was only when she was able to accept her own worthiness that she was able to feel true compassion for her own suffering. As Alice became more aware, her children were able to accept her back into their lives, and the lives of their own children, in a much more loving way.

Timing Is Important

Many clients report that it is essential that their therapists let them proceed at their own pace. As you progress in your therapy, things will come up that you're not quite ready to deal with head on. Remember, we often stay in the contemplation phase for some time, unable to move forward because of shame, anxiety, or guilt. Your therapist will do his best to earn your trust by not pushing you too fast or too hard.

Wendell described his late wife Barbara as a kind, patient, and wonderful person and himself as the sick one, always struggling with severe anxiety as well as anorexia. He never remembered a time in his life when he didn't feel very anxious, and his anorexia began soon after a period as a young teenager during which he was overweight. His weight became a reason for ongoing criticism and abuse from both his parents, whom he tried, but always seemed to fail, to please. In addition, his weight became fodder for relentless teasing and bullying by his peers.

It was unthinkable for him to imagine that Barbara, who indeed sounded wonderful, might not have been 100% perfect. His therapist, Zach, asked if she might have had some troubles of her own, but Wendell backed away from the question. Zach kept the question alive, occasionally inviting him to reconsider. One day Zach observed that Barbara had never said anything about either Wendell's anorexia or his anxiety. Wendell was ashamed of both conditions, especially the anorexia, typically considered a woman's problem. He always thought that Barbara was kind to put no pressure on him to change. He considered her acceptance of him, just as he was, extremely generous.

Now he began to wonder how she could have ignored his anorexia. She had known it put him in great danger. What was in it for her to express no concern? To turn a blind eye? Wendell recalled his female in-laws—his wife's two sisters and their mother. They also were perfect, patient women, married to men who seemed unable to take care of themselves. Zach speculated that the men agreed to take on the family pain, so that the women could be protected from it.

Zach also helped Wendell see that he had his own reasons for carrying all the pain and for idealizing his wife. His older sister had died in an accident when she was 10 and Wendell was 5. His parents never openly grieved their daughter's death and always spoke of her in glowing terms. They became increasingly distant with each other, focusing only on Wendell's problems with anxiety, weight, and then anorexia. In retrospect, it appeared that he played the role of the sick one in his family of origin as well as in his marriage, allowing his parents to avoid their grief. Furthermore, his idealization of Barbara mirrored the family's view of his older sister.

As sweet as Barbara was, Wendell slowly began to see how often they both did what she wanted. They moved often as she pursued her career as a professor, in spite of the fact that each move was a painful adjustment for Wendell and that Barbara already had a good teaching job in the city where they first met. Although he let her know he was unhappy, he was not very assertive about it, and she clearly missed the signal—even the signals of his increased anxiety and his deepening struggles with anorexia.

It was only when he began to see this dynamic that he was able to regard himself in a more compassionate light. He no longer had to define himself as the sick one in the relationship, grateful that his wife would put up with him. He still held a loving memory of her, but she was now someone with her own human frailties. And he, in turn, could see himself as someone with a large capacity to love and someone worthy of being loved.

Rhonda and Zach helped their clients move at a pace that they could tolerate. Zach gently invites his clients to explore an area by saying something like "Well, let's look at this." Rhonda's clients report that she communicates that gentle invitation with a look, a half smile, a cue that she thinks there's more here than meets the eye. They know she's on to something, but they don't feel pressure to go further than they can at the time.

Comfort is not the same thing as safety. Remember, a degree of stress, or discomfort, is necessary for growth and change to occur. So sometimes your therapist might be more forceful, strongly challenging you to move past your comfort zone. The things you discuss in therapy will often evoke painful feelings. Part of your therapist's job is to help you tolerate and work with those feelings.

How Do You Know Whom to Trust?

People come to therapy with prior experiences that shape their ideas about who is trustworthy and what constitutes trustworthy behavior. For those who come to therapy with little experience in trusting others, learning how and whom to trust will be a vital part of the work.

Some people worry that others will hurt them in some way if they share personal information. At worst, letting others know your inner life could lead to a punitive response, such as total rejection. If you have such concerns, it's hard to trust your therapist. Why should you? He's just there because it's his job. He doesn't care about you really. Who knows what his motive is? This very lack of trust can be an opening for you and your therapist. It may seem counterintuitive, but it can be the beginning of your exploration into how and when trust is possible.

When I discuss with clients the process of learning to trust, I tell them they first need to determine what to trust someone about. For example, I trust the mechanic next door to my office. He's honest and does good, reliable work on my car. Because I'm completely ignorant about the inner workings of cars, it's important to me that I can turn mine over to him without worrying that he'll cheat me. On what basis have I decided to trust him? First, I got a recommendation from a friend, whose judgment I trust. Then I noticed that he told me when something was and wasn't worth fixing. An untrustworthy mechanic could easily do unnecessary work on my car and get away with it. I wouldn't know the difference. Finally, when he's fixed a problem with my car, it stays fixed.

But I only trust him with my car. I don't trust him with my emotional struggles, and I probably never will. That's not his job and we're not friends.

We trust people on all sorts of levels, and it's not wise to trust them all the same way. We may have friends whom we trust to be on time, to meet their commitments to us, and to help us out in a pinch when we're in trouble. We need people in our lives whom we can trust in these ways. However, people who are trustworthy in these ways may not necessarily be trustworthy with our emotions, especially our fears. It requires a high level of trust to open our hearts. Some people simply aren't interested in such a close connection; others may hurt us—for example, by using what we share with them against us.

A crucial aspect of trust is the ability to trust yourself to determine whether others are trustworthy. If you can't trust yourself in this regard, then, of course, you'll be reluctant to open up with others. The experience of trusting a therapist can be the beginning of learning to how to do this.

When a client begins to trust me, I generally encourage him to explain why he does and what he trusts me to do. I ask him to articulate this so he can begin to notice what it's like to feel safe with someone, and so he can use that experience to discern whom in his life he can feel safe with and whom he can't.

For you to be able to trust your therapist, he needs to be compassionate, and he needs to hold you accountable in the ways I described in Chapter Nine. Both are necessary for your therapist to provide a safe environment, where you know you can be fully yourself and where you know, clearly, what the limits are. His compassion includes letting you know that he accepts you in your less-than-perfect emotional state. This means that if you're sad, confused, or rageful, even at him, he'll stick with you. He won't change the subject, fall asleep, or try to convince you that you shouldn't feel whatever it is you feel.

Accountability includes not letting you do anything that could be harmful to yourself or your work in therapy. This may require setting clear limits with you. For example, he may charge a fee if you don't show up for your appointments without reasonable notice. He may insist that you go to the hospital if you are unable to reassure him that you won't harm yourself. If you're there with your partner, he may not allow either of you to speak abusively to each other.

All therapists will not set the same limits. Some think it's useful, for example, to let a couple fight the way they do at home, even if it's verbally abusive (but not physically abusive; no one would allow physical violence to occur in a therapy session). The purpose of this is to see what really happens and then help clients deal with it. Some people believe that the manner in which you express your anger in the presence of your therapist offers an important piece of information and that it's important to let you do it however you do it. All good therapists, however, have bottom lines about what is acceptable and what is not—and they'll make those bottom lines very clear.

Finally, you need to trust that your therapist will not exploit you, that she will make every attempt to ensure that what she does is in your best interests. Because this is as much about power as it is about trust, we'll talk about it more in the next chapter.

If you don't trust your therapist but she passes all of the previous tests, your lack of trust may say more about you than her. You and your therapist can consider these questions: If you don't trust her, why not? What are you afraid she'll do or not do? What will happen to you if you open your heart to her? The answers to these questions will give you clues about what you bring to the table. You can begin to use your experience in therapy to examine your beliefs about whether or not you can count on others—and yourself.

As you read the next chapter on power and authority, you'll quickly see that there is a very strong relationship between power and trust. How you experience your therapist's use of power has everything to do with how much you trust him—and with how the therapeutic relationship evolves.

CHAPTER 12

Power and Authority

Unless your relationship with your therapist feels problematic in some way, you may not notice the roles that power and authority play in it. However, the one-way nature of the relationship means that your therapist has more power than you in many ways.

Psychotherapists, along with doctors, lawyers, teachers, and clergy, serve as members of the community from whom people seek guidance and help. This is the first element of the power imbalance between you and your therapist.[1]

What Does Your Therapist Know?

You'll remember from Chapter Two that 15% of the changes that result from a therapeutic relationship are based on hope. This means that you need to believe that your therapist can help. You need to have confidence that your therapist knows what she's doing and that, if she's confused about where to go next, she'll seek help to figure it out.

You probably assume, and reasonably so, that your therapist might know something about what's bothering you that you don't see yet. This doesn't mean she knows exactly how life is for you, but it does mean that she has some general ideas. For example, I came to understand anxiety, shame, and guilt through observation and experience; I have studied them a lot, talked and worked with many clients, and I have my own experiences with all three emotions.

Most clients don't care what type of therapeutic approach their therapist uses as long as it seems helpful. Most clients do care, however, whether their therapist has some knowledge about the issues they bring to the table. For example, a therapist may have a good deal of general knowledge and skill about the therapeutic process, but may not have worked with many people who share your particular issues and circumstances. You might not believe she is credible or useful unless she has that specialized expertise. And you might be right. For example, my colleague Gerry refers people with eating disorders to other professionals in the community who specialize in this area, because she feels she does not have the expertise to provide the best service.

However, no therapist knows everything. Any responsible therapist will consult with colleagues when he isn't sure what to do or thinks he doesn't know enough to work with you. In addition, therapists are always learning new things. The fact that your therapist doesn't know something that is relevant to you doesn't necessarily mean he can't work with you. He can often learn what he needs to learn in order to help you, either by seeking consultation or training or doing some reading.

WHAT YOU BRING TO THE TABLE: YOUR PAST EXPERIENCES

Your concerns about whether your therapist knows what she's doing, and your expectations of and reactions to your therapist regarding her knowledge, come through the lens of your experience. For example, if you expect people in charge to know everything and yourself to know nothing, then this is what you will initially expect of your therapist. On the other hand, if you expect people in charge to have little helpful knowledge and to be unable to give you useful guidance, you will (at least at first) have trouble accepting any suggestion your therapist might make.

"TELL ME WHAT TO DO"

Deo's family members were very involved in each other's lives. His father constantly gave him the message that he couldn't trust himself to know what to do. No matter the situation, he gave Deo a lot of unsolicited advice. If Deo had a problem with his house or car, his father made many comments implying that Deo was making poor decisions. At one point, when Deo was a graduate student, his father actually called the school, without Deo's knowledge or permission, to complain about a problem Deo was having with one of his professors.

Although Deo resented his father's attitude and experienced him as very intrusive, the message had its impact. Deo was virtually unable to make a decision without feeling extreme anxiety that whatever move he made was wrong. He relied heavily on his wife Lucy to make major decisions for the two of them. He even described sitting frozen in a restaurant, unable to decide what to order from the menu.

He came to therapy to address his general anxiety and to become more fully emancipated from his parents. Naturally, he ran into this issue in his relationship with his therapist, Fran. He frequently presented dilemmas to Fran, from whom he both sought and resisted advice. He wanted her to tell him what to do and would ask for her take on his decisions. If she offered suggestions, Deo felt controlled by her and perceived Fran as not trusting his ability to make his own decisions. On the other hand, if Fran took a neutral position, simply helping him sort out his internal competing forces, Deo would become very agitated, thinking that she expected something of him that he could not provide. He would become frozen, as he did in the restaurant, moving from worst-case scenario to worst-case scenario in his thinking, unable to find a way out of the trap of his anxiety.

Deo and Fran explored what was behind their interactions.

Fran: When you ask me for advice, what does it mean about you?

Deo: I feel like I don't know how to do it myself, so I have to ask. I don't trust myself.

Fran: So, then, when I make a suggestion . . .

Deo: It seems like you must agree. You don't think I can do it either.

Fran: So when I make a suggestion, I'm actually reinforcing your belief that you can't do it. It seems like it's equally difficult for you, though, when I don't make one—when I suggest that you brainstorm some ideas and look at the pros and cons of what you come up with. Do you have a sense of what happens for you then?

Deo: Then I start feeling like you don't care enough about me to help me out.

Fran: That's hard—really a bind. It seems that no matter how I respond,
        it doesn't help the anxiety. Is that true?

Deo: Yes . . . sometimes.

Fran: What do you say to yourself about that?

Deo: I must be right about my fears, if you can't help them go away. And
        then there's nothing I can do to prevent the worst-case scenario from
        occurring. It's hopeless.

Some people are less ambivalent than Deo about wanting to be told what to do. They may be temporarily confused and lost at a certain point in their lives. Or they may have a general belief that they are unable to figure out their own solutions and that others who are smarter or more capable or have more authority should tell them. Sometimes this comes from a cultural belief that the elders always know best.

Your therapist may indeed have some good ideas about what you should do. However, if you believe your therapist has all the answers, then he or she needs to challenge your belief. Most likely your therapist will resist taking on the job of finding your solutions for you; instead, he'll encourage you to create your own solutions. This doesn't mean that he will sit back and say nothing. He may ask you questions to help you identify possibilities and what you consider to be the risks and benefits of each of them. He may even suggest some possibilities himself, if you feel stuck, but rather than tell you which one is best, he'll help you determine that for yourself. He may explore with you how you came to believe that you had no ability to find your own answers. He may ask you to pay attention to what feelings and thoughts come up for you in reaction to his refusal to tell you what to do. As a consequence, you may find yourself feeling lost, angry, scared, or even betrayed. He may also ask you to explore what worries or frightens you about acting on your own behalf.

"DON'T TELL ME WHAT TO DO"

On the other end of the continuum are people who resist anything that seems like guidance from someone in a position of authority. Perhaps people who had authority in your life often gave you damaging guidance. Or maybe you have always had to take care of yourself. If so, the idea of relying on someone else feels dangerous, because the person could steer you in the wrong direction. You're unlikely to believe that your therapist's guidance is worth following. If you feel this way strongly, you probably got to therapy involuntarily in the first place. However, now that you're there, it's a good idea to consider what might be behind your reactions.

Suzanne's partner, Nadine, insisted that she go to therapy. Nadine was doing some personal work with another therapist and thought that Suzanne's inability to express her feelings in the relationship was a problem for them both. Suzanne didn't see the problem, but she loved Nadine and didn't want to lose her, so she agreed to go. Once in therapy, Suzanne became aware that she had always been her parents' confidante. They did not rely on each other for emotional support, nor did they have friends or others to whom they could go for guidance. Rather, they used their child.

Although this job was a burden for Suzanne, it was the only job she knew. Naturally, she repeated it in her friendships and in her relationship with Nadine. She could be counted on to listen and support them in all of their struggles, but she never asked for help or even shared her own.

Without knowing it, she carried a fear that if she didn't play this role, no one would value her friendship. In addition, because her parents switched roles with her, acting like children, expecting her to be the parent, Suzanne grew up believing she could not rely on others. Unconsciously, she felt she had only herself.

When she came to therapy, Suzanne found herself feeling very uncomfortable with being cared for, rather than caring for, the other person. How could she rely on someone else for that kind of help? Could her therapist really make any suggestions that would be worth exploring? On an unconscious level, she feared that her therapist would not want her around if she couldn't take care of him.

"I Know So Little about You, and You Know So Much about Me"

The one-way aspect of the therapeutic relationship means, among other things, that your therapist doesn't share his vulnerabilities with you. He does not ask you to help him cope with his struggles in life, whereas you are called upon to talk about things that are very personal to you. In fact, some people share even more personal information with their therapists than they do with their partners and closest friends. This imbalance causes some people a great deal of discomfort.

My client Margaux's family looked like the perfect family on the outside. Her father was a pastor with a large following of people who found him wise and understanding. Her mother was a warm and nurturing woman on whom many relied for comfort and companionship. Margaux's upper-middle-class home was filled with beauty, culture, and harmony. Nobody's feathers ever got ruffled. Why, she wondered, did she cry so easily, feel pain so deeply, and often find herself unhappy and confused? What was wrong with her?

Margaux told me, early on, that she had a lot of admiration for me. In her eyes, I seemed calm, wise, and understanding. Margaux put herself down in comparison to me. Clearly, she thought, I must have it all together, as her parents seemed to. I simply could not have the same struggles and doubts that Margaux experienced.

Margaux had mixed feelings about this phenomenon. On the one hand, she felt that she could learn from what she perceived as my better handle on life. On the other, this view of our differences reinforced her perception of her own inadequacies. This is not unusual. Clients often put their therapists on a pedestal, especially in the earlier stages of their work.

Idealizing someone is a natural way to develop a sense of who we want to be. As children we idealize our parents and often other adults in our world. We look up to them as people who will take care of us and who can do no wrong. As such, they help us feel safe in the world. And we begin to incorporate who they are into our own senses of self. As we mature, however, we begin to see their human frailties. By the time this happens, we have normally developed a strong enough sense of self so that we can accept both our parents' frailties and our own, and have confidence in our ability to survive and thrive in life.

When we engage in a new and scary venture as adults, we often feel the same insecurity we felt as children. We look to mentors who can help guide us. The younger we feel in our new venture, the more likely we are to perceive a big gap in competence between ourselves and our mentors, and the more likely we are to idealize them. When we begin therapy, we often feel quite young because we are entering new territory.

This phenomenon is enhanced by the difference in roles. Even though your therapist is acting in an authentic manner, she is only showing you certain aspects of herself. It's easy to assume that she doesn't have the kind of struggles that you do, especially if you are at a point in your relationship with yourself where you think your struggles are a sign of weakness rather than humanity.

For some people, being so much more vulnerable than their therapist is uncomfortable because, like Suzanne, they have never experienced it. They did not have parents or others whom they could idealize and rely on fully.

Therapists vary in the amount of personal information they share with their clients. Some share none or as little as possible. Others talk about being a parent, having a partner, their vacation plans, or other aspects of their lives, usually as a way of connecting with their clients or establishing shared meaning. A few share struggles they have had, if they think that doing so will affirm or normalize what the client is going through, or will communicate empathy or understanding. Your therapist might share something that worked for him that he thinks will work for you. However, the motive for your therapist's sharing is not to ask for your help in solving his problems. And, he is unlikely to share something about which he feels particularly raw unless he has no choice.

Pamela had no choice. Her husband had died in a community tragedy, and news of his death was in the paper. There was no way for her to keep this information from her clients, and no way for Pamela to deny her very raw feelings about it without being completely dishonest. However, she was acutely aware of the need to acknowledge her pain in a way that helped her clients and did not burden them with her grief. She did this in part by assuring her clients that she had a very strong group of friends and family who supported her. She was being cared for; this was not the client's job.

If you ask your therapist for personal information, she may tell you what you want to know, or she may say that this is not something she tells clients. Or, she may ask you to explore what it would mean to you to have the information. As in Suzanne's case, it may reveal something very important about your own situation. For Suzanne, learning how to let her therapist be someone on whom she could rely without having to take care of him emotionally was a very healing experience—one that helped her feel more compassion for herself and to trust the world just a little more.

The family role reversal is often less obvious than it was for Suzanne. Doug felt very close to both of his parents, who were loving and supportive. Yet, he was afraid to do anything that would upset them. He came to therapy because, although he was pursuing a college degree and getting good grades, he hated what he was doing. He wanted to quit and use the money he had saved to travel and figure out what he really wanted to do with his life. He knew his parents were extremely proud of him and would be disappointed if he left college. They had not gone to college, had worked hard to support Doug in going, and took great pleasure in his success. Adding to the pressure, Doug's older brother had never even finished high school or managed to find work that paid a living wage. Doug had always been the child who never caused his parents grief.

When Doug started therapy with Glen, he worked hard to anticipate what Glen thought he should do. He wanted to please Glen and went out of his way to do so. When they talked, Doug watched closely for any sign that Glen was uncomfortable with his decisions. At one point Glen did challenge him about a choice he'd made, but Doug disagreed with Glen's observations. Doug worried that Glen would not only be disappointed in him, but that he would hurt Glen's feelings by rejecting his advice. Doug didn't want Glen to feel bad about himself. If he did, Doug reasoned, Glen might be less interested in working with him. He might even refuse to continue the therapy. Although Doug was scared, he took the risk in the next session to say that he didn't accept Glen's opinion.

As they discussed his fear, Doug began to recognize that his parents were themselves very fearful and full of shame. He didn't want to cause them any more discomfort. He realized he was afraid that, if he did, they might not be able to tolerate it—and as a result, they wouldn't be able to be there for him. Children in this situation often feel like they have to hold up their parents so that their parents can do their job. Doug was worried that if he disappointed or hurt Glen, Glen would not be able to support him.

WHOSE NEEDS ARE WE MEETING HERE?

In general, it's the parent's job to meet the child's needs— not the reverse. Of course, in practice, children do meet many of their parents' needs, and as they mature, it's crucial that they understand that parents and others do have needs that children are obligated to consider. Children, however, should not have to make their parents feel okay in the world. Children should not have to parent their parents.

Over time, Doug learned that Glen could tolerate Doug's rejection of his suggestions. Glen didn't take it personally, didn't feel bad about himself. He would continue to be there for Doug and to engage in a genuine effort to help him. Learning this gave Doug the courage to explore what he wanted for himself in life, now knowing that he could do so without fear of losing Glen's support and guidance.

Doug's parents' behavior illustrates a relatively passive role reversal between parents and children. Because they didn't take care of their own needs, Doug's parents had abdicated their responsibility for meeting their children's emotional needs. It is more destructive when parents actively force their needs on their children through physical, sexual, or emotional abuse. Then children learn to fear people in power. They grow up expecting similar abuse from others. Sometimes they become abusive themselves as a method of self-protection. Sometimes they become submissive as a way to avoid the abuse. Sometimes they just shut down, refusing to let anyone close enough to hurt them.

When such adults get to therapy, they often assume that their therapist will hurt them in similar ways. Being asked to explore vulnerable parts of themselves can evoke feelings of fear and shame, and clients can easily begin to view therapists' encouragement to explore their vulnerability as attempts to hurt them.

As Suzanne continued in her therapy, she began to reveal that there was more to the story than that her parents relied on her as a confidante. In fact, her father had sexually abused her more than once and her mother had looked the other way, refusing to pick up on Suzanne's hints that she was afraid of her father. She had never shared this with anyone before, not even Nadine. Like many victims of sexual abuse, she felt deeply ashamed. She had concluded, as many children do, that if she were being hurt in this way, it must be because she was bad. And, like many children, she felt responsible, as if she should have been able to stop it. When she began to talk about this in therapy, she felt horribly exposed. She even felt as if her therapist took some perverse pleasure in hearing these painful details of her life. She became both angry and scared and, as she had always done, shut down to protect herself. It took a long time for her to recognize that her therapist was not using her for his own needs. He was letting her know that he could hear what had happened to her without turning away, like her mother had done. He knew that giving her the opportunity to talk about what had happened and how she felt would help her begin to heal a very deep wound.

BUT, ACTUALLY, THE POWER IS ALL YOURS

As we discussed earlier, in order for therapy to work, we must be open to examining and challenging our familiar ways of seeing and responding to things. If we aren't, we have no room to take in new information. This does not mean that it's necessary, or even a good idea, to believe everything your therapist says, do everything your therapist suggests, or talk about all the personal details of your life if you are reluctant to do so. You, not your therapist, are the expert on yourself and your own experience.

A big part of the work of therapy is learning to trust yourself. However, if you are not willing to seriously consider your therapist's ideas, and if you won't give your therapist important information about yourself, you won't progress. As our discussion here illustrates, when you don't want to do what your therapist suggests, you need to try to figure out whether your reluctance is because you are afraid or because your therapist's suggestion is not helpful or appropriate at this time.

A paradoxical interaction takes place between you and your therapist. In order to let the therapeutic process help you, you need to allow her to influence you. This gives her power in your life. At the same time, the power is actually entirely yours. You decide how much power to give her, how much to do in therapy, and whether to be there at all.

However, you probably won't think about the therapeutic relationship in terms of power, but in terms of trust. *I trust her wisdom. I trust her to have my best interests in mind. Therefore, I'll trust her with my heart.*

Alice, the client whose children had initially brought her to therapy to confront her about sexual abuse, was feeling suicidal. Initially she was afraid to tell her therapist Rhonda about it, because if she did, Rhonda might insist that she go to the hospital. However, by now she completely trusted Rhonda. She would go to the hospital if Rhonda told her to, even though she really didn't want to. At this point she would do anything Rhonda suggested, because she believed Rhonda saw things she didn't. By now she knew that Rhonda would never insist that she talk about something she wasn't ready for, but that Rhonda often picked up on something of importance that she herself hadn't noticed. She often wasn't sure which of her comments Rhonda would decide were important and worth exploring further, but the exploration kept proving worthwhile, so Alice's trust in Rhonda's ability to see what needed to happen and to guide her there continued to grow.

How do you know if you are giving your therapist too much power or not giving him enough? To help you decide, ask yourself these two questions: (1) Does what your therapist suggests help in the sense of pushing you in a direction that moves you toward greater awareness and personal responsibility? (2) Does it feel right? Again, "feel right" doesn't mean "feel comfortable." Much of therapy isn't comfortable. However, it should feel safe in the ways I described in the previous chapter. You should have a sense that your therapist is challenging you and supporting you at the same time. And you should have a sense that what you are doing is ultimately for you, not for him. If you are worried that your therapist needs you to act in some way in order to meet his needs, you should check that out with him and make sure that this is not the case. Like Suzanne, who worried that her therapist was doing so, it may take some time for you to be sure that he isn't. However, if you're confident that you've explored the issue, that you've ruled out the possibility that your feelings about this are more about your own past experience than about what your therapist is actually doing, then it's important to consider finding a new therapist.

"What If I Think I Need Something from My Therapist That He Won't Give Me?"

Sometimes the question of whether the therapy is meeting your needs or those of your therapist arises when you want something from your therapist that you know he won't give you. You may feel ashamed that you want it in the first place, or you may feel rejected because you can't have it.

Here's an important example. In the first two chapters of this book, I introduced Rachel, who at first would ask for, and then find ways to reject, her therapist Bob's help. As she became more and more able to open herself up to Bob, she found herself feeling sexually attracted to him. She wasn't sure how to handle these feelings. She felt like she was bad for having them. Yet she was aware of an intense desire to feel special in his eyes. If he were attracted to her as well, it would confirm that she was indeed special, not just another paying customer.

There's a lot tied up in the idea of being special. Remember that your therapist has a much bigger impact on your life than you do on his. You think about your therapy more than he does, and you care more about the outcome. That's how it should be. Your therapy is about your life, not your therapist's. However, for many people, this feels very uncomfortable, especially if they have not experienced being special to anyone. We all need the experience of being prized. As an old teacher of mine once said, everyone needs to be the light in his or her mother's eye. And, sadly, not everyone is. So we seek that experience elsewhere—often, for example, in our sexual partnerships. And it is possible, in fact, to find it there and heal that original wound.

So naturally, when we connect with a therapist and start sharing our most intimate selves, we want the therapist to feel as close to us as we do to him. The fact that he doesn't feel that way can make us feel unimportant. In addition, it's very natural to feel sexually attracted to someone with whom you feel safe, with whom you're sharing intimate details of your life. You might believe that being sexual with your therapist will make you feel truly special. And if you've had the experience of being sexually exploited by caregivers, you may believe that your sexuality is what makes you valuable as a person.

I've only named here some of the possibilities of what your feelings might mean. Should you feel this way about your therapist, he should be able to respond in a way that:

- Lets you know that the feelings are okay for you to have.
- Gives you space and permission to explore what they signify.
- Lets you know that, no matter what, he won't act on them or let you act on them.

This is a promise that he will keep you safe.

This is what I say to a client who is having these feelings:

The relationship between therapist and client is a sacred one, similar to the relationship between a parent and child. Being a child is, in and of itself, to be in a privileged position. If you are "more than a child" to your parent, a sacred bond is broken. You are meeting a need for your parent that you shouldn't be meeting. The same is true for the therapist–client relationship. Being "only" my client doesn't make you ordinary, and it certainly doesn't mean that I don't care deeply about you.

It does mean I will not sacrifice our relationship by making it something that it isn't. I keep and guard this boundary so that you can be safe. You don't have to worry that I will use what you are experiencing for my needs. I will use it only for yours. Therefore, you are free to experience your feelings to their fullest and to explore their meaning with me without worry about what will happen to you or our relationship in the process.

A SHIFT IN THE BALANCE OF POWER

Over time, your experience of the imbalance of power between you and your therapist will begin to shift. You will become more and more aware that your therapist is simply another human being, equal to you as a person, unequal because of the roles you each play in the relationship. Margaux, who originally thought she was weak in comparison to me, later went through a profound evolution. Her next stage was to depersonalize me. She thought of me almost in objectified terms. I was a helpful resource that Margaux could count on when she needed some input. I'll be there, in my office at the appointed time, ready to listen.

A third stage occurred when I was leaving town during a particularly intense phase of Margaux's work. I told her that she would be in my heart, a comment intended to let her know that our bond continued, even if we couldn't meet for a few weeks. The comment surprised Margaux. She hadn't realized that I cared about her, although we'd worked together a number of times over many years. Initially, she was quite uncomfortable with the idea. When we explored her discomfort, Margaux identified her worry that if I cared about her, I would expect something from her. For Margaux, caring from the adults in her life had come with a big price tag. Her realization that I could just care, and that she could just be herself, was an important step toward caring for herself in a fuller way.

By the end of our work together, Margaux had reached yet another stage. At this point she viewed us as two women, both walking through life together. Had we met under different circumstances, we might have been friends. But the roles we played, mine as therapist and Margaux's as client, afforded us a unique and special relationship, one that nurtured us both in different ways.

By now I hope you have a good idea about the many things you might experience in this very fascinating journey called psychotherapy, and how you can use this process to its fullest potential. In the final chapter, we'll consider bringing your therapy to a close, how you might recognize that it's time to do so, and how to use that closing to enhance your growth.

CHAPTER 13

Saying Goodbye

E nding therapy is a very important part of the overall therapeutic process. Often, clients are unsure about whether they are ready to leave, and sometimes have strong and conflicting feelings about doing so. As with other aspects of the therapy experience, you may find yourself feeling and behaving the way you did when other important relationships in your life came to an end. Because leaving or losing relationships is often difficult, saying goodbye to your therapist—and to the therapeutic process—may be challenging as well. In this chapter, we'll discuss some common issues that arise. It will become clear that careful attention to how you end your therapy can contribute to the overall quality of the experience, and to your growth.

"How Do I Know I'm Ready?"

Ideally, but not necessarily, you will end your therapy because you're done with your work and satisfied with what you got out of the process. Given that life continually presents us with new challenges, how do you know if you're done? Revisiting your goals can help. Has your depression lifted to the point where you feel more hopeful about life? Are you more able to identify and express your feelings, needs, and desires? Do you set more effective limits with your children? Have you developed useful coping strategies to manage your angry outbursts, your panic or anxiety, or your shame? Do you and your partner treat each other with more compassion and have a clearer understanding of how to address your differences?

Sometimes clients just know they are ready. They find themselves coming to sessions with less to say, or reporting on things they've already figured out rather than asking for the therapist's help. Or they start regarding their therapy appointments as an interruption, something that seems to get in the way of doing what they really want to do with their day. Sometimes they begin to have trouble making the appointments at all.

If I notice such changes in a client's behavior, I know we have something we need to address. That something may be that the client is done. The time is simply not as important as it was because the client doesn't feel the need for it anymore. Maybe she wants to continue for a little while longer, but meeting less frequently, perhaps once every month or 2 months. She may not have articulated that realization to herself or to me in an overt way, or she may be concerned about how I'll react to the idea, so she's sending the message indirectly.

"But Maybe I'm Missing Something, after All"

Of course, some people want to end therapy because they are reluctant, or scared, to stay and take the next step. If you make a sudden decision to stop, it might be because of this type of reluctance. Maybe you're aware of a vague, unsettled feeling in your stomach. Maybe you're thinking that your therapist isn't telling you anything useful or new or is on the wrong track. If you notice this happening to you, it's useful to ask yourself if something is happening in the therapy that's making you uncomfortable.

The issue may sometimes be fairly obvious, at least in retrospect. Myra recently started talking with her therapist about the fact that she'd been thinking she might be a lesbian, and then got scared of what that could mean if it were really true. For a few weeks Geoff had been discussing the idea of asking his parents to join him for some family sessions but then began to think it was just not necessary. Still, he felt that his therapist Melissa would want him to do it.

Whatever the situation, I encourage you to let your therapist know what you're thinking, so that you can take a look, together, at what might be going on. If you don't, you may miss an opportunity for some important work.

Geoff did go back to his therapist and together, they quickly identified his concern. This became an opportunity for Geoff to check out his assumptions, something he generally didn't do in his relationships. He learned that he was correct: Melissa did think meeting with his parents was a good idea. However, she didn't think it necessary to his progress, and she certainly wouldn't insist that he do so if he didn't want to. As with many people who are ambivalent about something, Geoff had assigned Melissa one side of the question so he could argue with someone other than himself, rather than tolerate the discomfort of his own internal debate.

Geoff and Melissa explored his reluctance to ask his parents to join them, as well as the potential benefits of doing
so. They talked about what the agenda would be and what
roles both Geoff and Melissa would play in the sessions. It
emerged that Geoff was afraid that Melissa would expect
him to tell his parents all of the ways he felt they had failed
him as a child. He didn't think this would do anything but
hurt them.

But Melissa had no such agenda in mind. She was clear
with Geoff that, at this point, his parents were coming to help
him with his therapy. They had not decided to be clients
themselves. She felt it would be appropriate for him to talk
with his parents about current concerns that were causing
some strain for him. She saw her job as helping Geoff identify what he would like his relationship with his parents to
be and to state his wishes for such a relationship in a respectful manner. If both Geoff and his parents agreed to do so,
they might also, in a later session, explore their past history
together.

Finally, it's possible that your therapist will conclude that
it's a good idea for you to end your therapy even though you
haven't come to that conclusion yourself. This could occur if
she sees that you have done the work you came to do, but you
haven't yet given yourself credit for your accomplishments.
It could also occur if she thinks you aren't prepared to do the
necessary work. Perhaps, for example, you've missed several
appointments, have little to talk about in therapy, and can't
identify (or don't want to explore) the meaning behind your
actions. Meanwhile, your actions don't change. She might,
in this case, suggest that you take some time off to think

about whether therapy is something you really want to do at
this point in your life.

"Or Maybe My Therapist Is Missing Something"

Some people decide that they want to end therapy because
they don't think the process is working. If you think this is
your situation, it's still worth talking about it with your therapist. Maybe your therapist is missing something important
that, together, you can address.

Sohela was unhappy with her therapist. Both lived in a
small Iranian-American community. But Sohela never talked
about the fact that, because her therapist Lili was also Iran-
ian, Muslim, and a woman, she reminded Sohela of her
mother, whom she could never trust to keep a confidence.
Sohela's discomfort was exacerbated by her frequent chance
encounters with Lili in the community. Sohela was never
sure that Lili could refrain from telling others about their
relationship.

Behind this was deeper concern. Sohela had been sexually
abused by her uncle and, through therapy, was slowly coming
to terms with the experience. Her approach to therapy had
always been to come in, do a bit of work, leave for a while,
and then return to do a bit more. Lili didn't challenge this
pattern, thinking that it was important to honor Sohela's
pace in dealing with her pain. Sohela heard about her
friend's Christian therapist and found herself thinking she
would prefer to work with that therapist instead of with Lili.

Only then did they discuss Sohela's concerns. Lili's acceptance of Sohela's starting and stopping therapy had led Sohela to think that Lili wasn't taking seriously how painful
the sexual abuse had been. Sohela's mother had always told

Sohela's aunts everything about Sohela, who was often quite embarrassed when her aunts would tease her about it. She had kept the abuse a secret for this very reason. She dreaded the possibility that her mother would minimize it and even share it as gossip.

Lili had clearly missed something important. However, Sohela's feedback allowed them to get back on track. The fact that Sohela could address and work through her concerns with Lili strengthened her trust in Lili to take her concerns seriously and to keep their relationship, and their work together, private and safe.

It's possible that you may decide, after bringing up your concerns, that your initial plan to leave was right. Sometimes, even if you and your therapist work hard, you don't make as much progress as both of you think you could. It may be that another therapist's style or approach to therapy would be a better fit for you. Your therapist is ethically obligated to do whatever she can to help you continue your work if, for any reason, the therapy ends before the work is done. By bringing up your concerns, among other things, you give yourself the opportunity to get some referrals to other therapists.

If you are not satisfied with the way your therapist responds to your concerns, it may well be appropriate to end the relationship. Perhaps you feel that your therapist doesn't make the effort to really understand what's bothering you. Perhaps even if he seems to see your point, nothing really changes.

Nate and Lanna had seen Mick for couples therapy for 2 months, but didn't think things were changing for the better in their relationship. Lanna thought Mick sided too often with Nate; he rarely seemed to see her point of view. Even Nate acknowledged that he didn't think Mick challenged him enough. They brought it up in therapy, but Mick didn't seem to take their concern very seriously. Although he acknowledged that this might be the case, he also defended what he had done. The dynamic didn't change, and neither did Nate and Lanna's relationship. Nate and Lanna decided it was, indeed, a good idea to stop seeing Mick, and they felt confident in their decision to find another therapist.

Ending Therapy before You're Ready

People also end therapy for reasons having nothing to do with the therapeutic process. You may move or have some personal situation that makes it difficult to continue; your therapist may leave her job or retire; or your insurance coverage may end.

If you're leaving because of a decision you have made—for example, you have accepted a job in another city—you may regret having to stop your therapy before you're ready, and it may be difficult to consider continuing your work with someone else. But it can be more challenging if your therapist leaves her practice or moves. You may experience her as abandoning you, even if you know that her leaving has nothing to do with you. You may be angry because you are helpless to do anything about it.

You might have similar feelings about losing your insurance coverage. Some therapists can negotiate a reduced sliding fee to enable you to continue, but many will not or cannot.

If you want to continue in therapy, your therapist will try to help you find a way to do that. If your therapist is leaving, perhaps there is another person in the same clinic who can see you or someone else in town whom your therapist can recommend. If your insurance coverage stops, perhaps you can find a therapist who provides services at a reduced fee. Perhaps there is a group in the community that will support you as you continue your therapeutic work.

It's possible that shifting to a different therapist will benefit you in ways you can't predict. Doing another leg of your journey with another therapist, despite the disappointment and disruption, can often offer a fresh and valuable challenge.

Julie started her therapy with Margaret, but after Margaret finished an internship at the agency, Julie transferred to Victoria. Julie had done very good work with Margaret. Because Julie and Margaret were the same age, Julie thought of Margaret as more of a friend and had connected easily with her. But as Julie got deeper into her work with Victoria, an older, motherly woman, she found it easier to be vulnerable with her. Victoria offered wisdom that comes with age, and her style, which was gentler than Margaret's, helped Julie feel safer. Julie later speculated, however, that had she stayed with Margaret, she would have been able to go into deeper water with her as well. She concluded that her work with both women was very successful.

"UH-OH! AM I REALLY READY?"

Sometimes in anticipating ending therapy, clients find themselves feeling or acting the way they did when they began the process.

Recall Doug from the previous chapter, who was initially afraid to disagree with his therapist Glen for fear that he would hurt Glen's feelings. He discovered that he had always taken care of his parents' feelings and assumed he had to do the same with Glen. Although he made much progress on this issue, and now had both the confidence and the ability to identify his feelings and needs, he found himself afraid to tell Glen that he was ready to leave therapy. He feared that Glen would be hurt. He worried about whether Glen would fill his usual time slot, whether Glen would be able to pay his bills. As they discussed his concern, Doug recognized his old pattern of unnecessary caretaking.

This return of a pattern thought to be resolved can be somewhat alarming. If this happens to you, you may worry that you've wasted your time. Take heart. This is not the case. More likely, you just feel some anxiety about whether you can continue the work on your own. This phenomenon usually passes quickly, with the client soon feeling much more confident about ending the work.

"What if I Want to Come Back?"

Some people want to know whether it is okay to return to therapy at a later time, either the same or a different therapist, and what it would mean to do so. It's almost always okay to return to therapy if you want to do more work. (However, your medical insurance may no longer cover your therapy; check with your insurer.) You can usually return to the same therapist unless he is unavailable.

A common misperception is that returning to therapy means that you failed to make the changes you wanted to make, that you have regressed, or that you were wrong about your ability to make it on your own. Although these are all possibilities, there is another, much more likely explanation for the desire to return: Your therapist was helpful, and you want to consult her again to help you deal with a new challenge.

How Is This Ending Different from Others?

Many of us have mixed feelings about saying goodbye to friends, relatives, or others in our lives. Often we end relationships because they are bad for us, or because we've lost interest. We do not ordinarily end personal relationships because they have gone well or been successful. Thus, ending successful therapy is typically bittersweet. We celebrate an accomplishment, but have to leave a relationship that was positive and nurturing in significant ways, simply because the work we came to do is done.

Why Is It So Important to Talk about Ending?

Whatever the reason for ending the relationship, talking about it with your therapist rather than simply going away is important. First, acknowledging the end honors the relationship and the work that you did together. Doing therapy takes a great deal of courage and commitment on your part. To fail to acknowledge it sells yourself, your relationship with your therapist, and the therapeutic process short.

As with other phases of the therapeutic process, the way we view saying goodbye is shaped by our past experiences. I have often had clients tell me in our first meeting that when things get hard in relationships, their usual habit is to leave. When I hear this, I say to them, "If you ever start to feel like that in our relationship, please talk to me about it before you leave. The therapeutic relationship is a unique opportunity to gain new awareness about how you operate in the world and to practice new skills. Because therapy is challenging work, at some point we'll run up against something that's very difficult. When this happens, please don't just go away. Call me."

By asking for this promise, I challenge people whose automatic response is to avoid discomfort or pain. If they do later feel tempted to bail out of therapy, I remind them of their promise.

As you prepare to leave therapy, you may find yourself remembering some of your past experiences with ending relationships and the feelings that accompanied those experiences. Talking about these in therapy offers you the opportunity to revisit and resolve feelings about those other partings. This can help heal old wounds.

A thoughtful ending allows for a review of your progress— what worked and what did not, and where you want to go from here. Even if you didn't work with your therapist for very long, a short conversation reviewing what you did together can be useful. You can articulate and discuss the changes you have made and get feedback. You might hear how much your therapist valued his time with you. You might pose questions you were reluctant to ask earlier or didn't think to raise before.

Saying goodbye to your therapist in a complete and constructive manner—one that does not leave you with unfinished business—can be a corrective experience that will, in itself, be healing.

As we say goodbye to one another, I want to wish you well on your journey. As you move through the therapeutic process and into yourself, you will discover new and interesting territory, and revisit old familiar places with new eyes. If you use your psychotherapy for all it's worth, you will learn to live in your life with an awareness that keeps expanding to meet new possibilities and new challenges. You will discover the fullness of life.

BOOKS YOU MIGHT WANT TO READ

Recommendations from Therapists and Clients

Abrahms, J., & Spring, M. (1996). *After the affair.* New York: Harper Collins.

Alberti, R. E., & Emmons, M. L. (1986). *Your perfect right: A guide to assertive living.* San Luis Obispo, CA: Impact.

Bass, E., & Davis, L. (1988). *The courage to heal: A guide for women survivors of child sexual abuse.* New York: Perennial Library.

Boss, P. (1999). *Ambiguous loss: Learning to live with unresolved grief.* Cambridge, MA: Harvard University Press.

Bireda, M. (1990). *Love addiction: A guide to emotional independence.* Oakland, CA: New Harbinger.

Burns, D. (1980). *Feeling good: The new mood therapy.* New York: Morrow.

Bloomfield, H. H., Colgrove, M., & McWilliams, P. (2000). *How to survive the loss of a love.* Allen Park, MI: MaryBooks.

Brown, B. (2007). *I thought it was just me: Women reclaiming power and courage in a culture of shame.* New York: Gotham Books.

Davis, L., (1990). *The courage to heal workbook: For women and men survivors of child sexual abuse.* New York: Perennial Library.

Emmons, H. (2006). *The chemistry of joy: A three-step program for overcoming depression through Western science and Eastern wisdom.* New York: Fireside.

Epstein, M. (1998). *Going to pieces without falling apart: A Buddhist perspective on Wholeness.* New York: Broadway Books.

Forward, S., & Frazier, D. (1997). *Emotional blackmail: When the people in your life use fear, obligation, and guilt to manipulate you.* New York: Harper Collins.

Fossom, M., & Mason, M. (1986). *Facing shame: Families in recovery.* New York: Norton.

Goldhor Lerner, H. (1985). *The dance of anger: A woman's guide to changing the patterns in intimate relationships.* New York: Harper & Row.

Goldhor Lerner, H. (1989). *The dance of intimacy: A woman's guide to courageous acts of change in key relationships.* New York: Harper & Row.

Gottman, J. M., Gottman, J. S., & DeClaire, J. (2006). *Ten lessons to transform your marriage: America's love lab experts share their strategies for strengthening your relationship.* New York: Crown.

Gottman, J., & Silver, N. (1999). *The seven principles for making marriage work.* New York: Crown.

Kirshenbaum, M. (1996). *Too good to leave, too bad to stay: A step-by-step guide to help you decide whether to stay in or get out of your relationship.* New York: Crown.

Kreger, R., & Shirley, J. P. (2002). *The stop walking on eggshells workbook: Practical strategies for living with someone who has borderline personality disorder.* Oakland, CA: New Harbinger.

Mason, P. T., & Kreger, R. (1998). *Stop walking on eggshells.* Oakland, CA: New Harbinger.

Mellody, P., Wells, A., & Miller, K. (1992). *Facing love addiction: Giving yourself the power to change the way you love: The love connection to codependence.* New York: Harper.

Real, T. (1997). *I don't want to talk about it: Overcoming the secret legacy of male depression.* New York: Scribner.

Richo, D. (1991). *How to be an adult: A handbook on psychological and spiritual integration.* New York: Paulist Press.

Richo, D. (2002). *How to be an adult in relationships: The five keys to mindful loving.* Boston: Shambhala.

Notes

Chapter One

1. Breuer, J., & Freud, S. (1957). *Studies on hysteria*. New York: Basic Books. This is an English translation of a book written by Breuer and Freud in 1895 that is considered the first book on psychoanalysis.

2. Psychotherapists are mandated reporters. This means that if they learn that a client has hurt a child or a vulnerable adult, they have to report the person to the county's child or adult protection agency. Therapists are also obligated to warn anyone whom they have good reason to believe their clients intend to hurt. In addition, if they have good reason to believe a client might hurt him- or herself, they need to do everything they can to prevent that from happening. This could include telling someone in the client's family or, in extreme cases, calling the police. Finally, if a client is involved in a court case, it's possible that the court would subpoena his therapy records.

3. Chiles, J. A., Lambert, M. J., & Hatch, A. L. (1999). The impact of psychological interventions on medical cost offset: A meta-analytic review. *Clinical Psychology: Science and Practice, 6*(2), 204–220.

Pennebaker, J. W., Kiecolt-Glaser, J., & Glaser, R. (1988). Disclosure of traumas and immune function: Health implications for psychotherapy. *Journal of Consulting and Clinical Psychology, 56*, 239–245.

Cohen, S., Tyrrell, D. A., & Smith, A. P. (1991). Psychological stress and susceptibility to the common cold. *New England Journal of Medicine, 325,* 606–612.

Luborsky, L. (1996). *The symptom–context method: Symptoms as opportunities in psychotherapy.* Washington, DC: American Psychological Association.

Compas, B. E., Haaga, D. A. F., Keefe, F. J., Leitenberg, H., & Williams, D. A. (1998). Sampling of empirically supported psychological treatments from health psychology: Smoking, chronic pain, cancer, and bulimia nervosa. *Journal of Consulting and Clinical Psychology, 66,* 89–112.

CHAPTER TWO

1. Bergin, A. E. (1971). The evaluation of therapeutic outcomes. In A. E. Bergin & S. L. Garfield (Eds.), *Handbook of psychotherapy and behavior change* (pp. 217–270). New York: Wiley.

Smith, M. L., Glass G. V., & Miller, T. I. (1980). *The benefits of psychotherapy.* Baltimore: Johns Hopkins University Press.

Lambert, M. J., & Bergin, A. E. (1994). In A. E. Bergin & S. L. Garfield (Eds.), *Handbook of psychotherapy and behavior change* (4th ed., pp. 143–189). New York: Wiley.

Seligman, M. E. P. (1995). The effectiveness of psychotherapy: The Consumer Reports study. *American Psychologist. 50*(12), 965–974.

Wampold, B. (2001). *The great psychotherapy debate.* Hillsdale, NJ: Erlbaum.

2. Duncan, B., Miller, S., & Sparks, J. (2004). *The heroic client: A revolutionary way to improve effectiveness through outcome-informed therapy.* San Fransisco: Jossey-Bass.

Information for the rest of this chapter is taken from Hubble, J., Duncan, B., & Miller, S. (Eds.). (1999). *The heart and soul of change: What works in therapy.* Washington, DC: American Psychological Association.

3. This section is based on the work of Tallman, K., & Bohart, A. (1999). The client as a common factor: Clients as self-healers. In J. Hubble, B. Duncan, & S. Miller (Eds.), *The heart and soul of change: What works in therapy* (pp. 91–131). Washington, DC: American Psychological Association.

4. This section is based on the work of Bachelor, A., & Horvath, A. (1999). The therapeutic relationship. In J. Hubble, B. Duncan, & S. Miller (Eds.), *The heart and soul of change: What works in therapy* (pp. 133–178). Washington, DC: American Psychological Association.

5. This section is based on the work of Snyder, C. R., Michel, S. C., & Cheavens, J. S. (1999). Hope as a psychotherapeutic foundation of common factors, placebos, and expectancies. In J. Hubble, B. Duncan, & S. Miller (Eds.), *The heart and soul of change: What works in therapy* (pp. 179–200). Washington, DC: American Psychological Association.

6. This section is based on the work of Ogles, B., Anderson, T., & Lunmen, K., (1999). The contribution of models and techniques to therapeutic efficacy: Contradictions between professional trends and clinical research. In J. Hubble, B. Duncan, & S. Miller (Eds.), *The heart and soul of change: What works in therapy* (pp. 201–225). Washington, DC: American Psychological Association.

7. Weber, S. (1996). The effects of relaxation exercises on anxiety levels in psychiatric inpatients. *Journal of Holistic Nursing, 14*(3), 196–205.

CHAPTER THREE

1. Cozolino, L. (2002). *The neuroscience of psychotherapy.* New York: Norton.

2. Johnson, H. C. (2004). *Psyche and synapse expanding worlds: The role of neurobiology in emotions, behavior, thinking and addiction for non-scientists* (2nd ed.). Greenfield, MA: Deerfield Valley.

Nasir, H., Naqvi, B., & Damasio, A. (2007). Damage to the insula disrupts addiction to cigarette smoking. *Science, 26,* 531–534.

3. Seigel, D. J. (1999). *The developing mind: How relationships and the brain interact to shape who we are.* New York: Guilford Press.

Bowlby, J. (1969). *Attachment and loss: Attachment* (Vol. 1). New York: Basic Books.

Ainsworth, M. D. S., Blehar, M. C., Waters, E., & Wall, S. (1978). *Patterns of attachment: A psychological study of the strange situation.* Hillsdale, NJ: Erlbaum.

Chapter Four

1. Scharff, K. (2004). *Therapy demystified: An insider's guide to getting the right help (without going broke)* (pp. 5 & 6). New York: Marlowe & Company.

2. American Psychological Association (2000). Diagnostic and statistical manual of mental disorders: DSMIVTR. Washington, DC: American Psychological Association.

3. Morrison, J. (2002). *Straight talk about your mental health: Everything you need to know to make smart decisions.* New York: Guilford Press.

Chapter Five

1. "Shared meaning" is a term developed by Sherod Miller, Daniel Wackman, and Elan Nunnally (1975), who created a strategy to help people

improve their communication skills, (*Alive and aware: Improving communication in relationships*, Minneapolis: Interpersonal Communication Programs). In my 1997 book *Supervisory relationships: Exploring the human element* (Pacific Grove, CA: Brooks/Cole), I named shared meaning, trust, and power as the primary elements of the relationship between therapists and their supervisors. The same elements are core to the relationship between clients and their therapists as well.

2. Gumperz, J. J. (1979). *Crosstalk.* London: British Broadcasting Corporation, Continuing Education Department, National Centre for Industrial Language Training.

3. Bachelor, A. (1988). How clients perceive therapist empathy: A content analysis of "received" empathy. *Psychotherapy: Theory, Research and Practice, 25*, 227–240.

CHAPTER SIX

1. The two major schools of current thought are object relations, initially proposed by Melanie Klein (1964, *Contributions to psychoanalysis, 1921–1945*; New York: McGraw-Hill), and self psychology, introduced by Heinz Kohut (1971, *The analysis of the self*; New York: International Universities Press, and [1977] *The restoration of the self,* New York: International Universities Press).

"Object relations" means relationships with others. In the context of this theory, the word *object* means the focus of a person's emotional investment, in this case, another person. The theory is based on the premise that attachment to parents or other early caretakers is essential for psychological and even physical survival. In addition, our experience of those early relationships is extremely influential in shaping the ways in which we see ourselves and others.

Self psychology is based on the premise that the development of a strong sense of self requires three essential aspects. The first is the experience of being deeply understood and feeling highly prized, or special, in the eyes of our caregivers. This experience tells us we are lovable for who we are. The second, having caregivers whom we can admire, gives us positive role models whose values and actions we can make our own. Finally, we need to experience a sense of belonging, which we gain by seeing that we are "like" others in our family and community.

2. Erikson, E. (1964). *Childhood and society.* New York: Norton.

3. The two most influential thinkers behind behavior theory are Ivan Pavlov and Burrhus F. Skinner. Pavlov is famous for his experiment with dogs, in which he demonstrated that dogs not only salivated in the presence of food, but in the presence of the person who was associated with giving the food. This discovery led to the principle behind "classical conditioning," whereby behavior is elicited by specific stimuli. Skinner is famous for his experiments on "operant conditioning," whereby consequences, such as reinforcement or punishment, are used to modify or extinguish behavior altogether.

Aaron Beck, considered the "father of cognitive therapy," began his research in 1959 and has published more than 450 articles and 17 books. He was the first to establish the efficacy of any psychotherapy for the treatment of depression.

4. Donald Meichenbaum is considered a major theorist in the development of the cognitive–behavioral approach. Meichenbaum's 1977 book (*Cognitive–behavior modification: An integrative approach*; New York: Plenum Press) is considered a classic in the field.

5. Research has documented that cognitive–behavioral interventions do indeed change brain functioning. See e.g., Schwartz, J. M. (1996). *Brain lock: Free yourself from obsessive–compulsive behaviors.* New York: Regan Books.

6. This chart is taken from Greenberg, D., & Padeskly, C. (1995). *Mind over mood: Change how you feel by changing the way you think*. New York: Guilford Press.

7. This concept is considered the peak of what Abraham Maslow called human beings' "hierarchy of needs," which begins with basic physiological needs such as for food and sleep. Maslow, A. (1943). A theory of human motivation. *Psychological Review*, *50*, 370–96.

8. Carl Rogers, considered the "father of client-centered therapy," wrote two seminal books on the topic: *Client-centered therapy: Its current practice, implications, and theory*. (1951). Boston: Houghton Mifflin, and *On becoming a person: A therapist's view of psychotherapy*. (1961). Boston: Houghton Mifflin.

9. Gestalt therapy was first described in Perls, F., Goodman, P., & Hefferline, R. (1951). *Gestalt therapy: Excitement and growth in the human personality*. New York: Dell.

10. The major schools of family systems therapy include:

- *Intergenerational*
  Bowen, M. (1978). *Family therapy in clinical practice*. New York: Aronson.

- *Structural*
  Minuchin, S. (1974). *Families and family therapy*. Cambridge, MA: Harvard University Press.

- *Strategic*
  Haley, J. (1976). *Problem solving in therapy: New strategies for effective family therapy*. San Francisco: Jossey-Bass.
  Madoness, C. (1981). *Strategic family therapy*. San Francisco: Jossey-Bass.

- *Humanistic*
  Satir, V. (1983). *Conjoint family therapy* (3rd ed.). Palo Alto, CA: Science and Behavior Books.

- *Experiential*
  Whitaker, C. & Malone, T. (1981). *The roots of psychotherapy.* New York: Brunner/Mazel.

- *Solution-Oriented*
  DeShazer, S. (1985). *Keys to solutions in family therapy.* New York: Norton.

- *Narrative*
  White M. & Epston, D. (1990). *Narrative means to therapeutic ends.* New York: Norton.

Chapter Eight

1. Prochaska, J., Norcross, J., & DiClemente, C. (1994). *Changing for good.* New York: Avon Books.

2. Greenberger, D., & Padesky, C. A. (1995). *Mind over mood: Change how you feel by changing the way you think.* New York: Guilford Press.

3. Stuart, R. (1980). *Helping couples change: A social learning approach to marital therapy.* New York: Guilford Press.

4. Luepker, E. (2003). *Record keeping in psychotherapy and counseling.* New York: Brunner-Routledge. Luepker gives clinicians a practical guide for record keeping, suggesting, among other things, that doing so can be helpful for clients in the ways I describe here.

5. Preston, J., & Johnston, J. (2007). *Clinical psychopharmacology made ridiculously simple* (5th ed.). Miami: MedMaster.

Chapter Ten

1. The term *shame-based* comes from the chemical dependency field and describes those who organize their lives around avoiding and

responding to shame. I have applied this dynamic to those who do the same thing with anxiety and guilt, calling such behavior *anxiety-based* and *guilt-based*.

2. Kubler-Ross, E. (1969). *On death and dying.* New York: Macmillan. Kubler-Ross proposed five stages of grieving, starting with "denial" and resolved with "acceptance."

3. Kaufman, G. (1980). *Shame: The power of caring.* Cambridge, MA: Schenkman.

CHAPTER TWELVE

1. Peterson, M. (1992). *At personal risk: Boundary violations in professional–client relationships.* New York: Norton. Marilyn Peterson, a therapist and teacher of therapists, is a leader in the field on the topic of boundary violations. She notes that the power differential between professionals and their clients, students, parishioners, or patients can set the stage for boundary violations if the professionals either exploit their power or fail to acknowledge it and use it responsibly.

INDEX